WITHDRAWN

Excel Pivot Tables Recipe Book

A Problem-Solution Approach

DEBRA DALGLEISH

Apress®

Excel Pivot Tables Recipe Book: A Problem-Solution Approach

Copyright © 2006 by Debra Dalgleish

ISBN-13 (pbk): 978-1-59059-629-6

ISBN-10 (pbk): 1-59059-629-3

Printed and bound in the United States of America 9 8 7 6 5 4 3 2

Lead Editor: Ewan Buckingham
Technical Reviewer: Don Reamy
Editorial Board: Steve Anglin, Dan Appleman, Ewan Buckingham, Gary Cornell, Jason Gilmore, Jonathan Hassell, James Huddleston, Chris Mills, Matthew Moodie, Dominic Shakeshaft, Jim Sumser, Matt Wade
Project Manager: Kylie Johnston
Copy Edit Manager: Nicole LeClerc
Copy Editor: Liz Welch
Assistant Production Director: Kari Brooks-Copony
Production Editor: Katie Stence
Compositor: Kinetic Publishing Services, LLC
Proofreader: Elizabeth Berry
Indexer: Valerie Perry
Cover Image Designer: Kurt Krames
Manufacturing Director: Tom Debolski

Distributed to the book trade worldwide by Springer-Verlag New York, Inc., 233 Spring Street, 6th Floor, New York, NY 10013. Phone 1-800-SPRINGER, fax 201-348-4505, e-mail orders-ny@springer-sbm.com, or visit http://www.springeronline.com.

For information on translations, please contact Apress directly at 2560 Ninth Street, Suite 219, Berkeley, CA 94710. Phone 510-549-5930, fax 510-549-5939, e-mail info@apress.com, or visit http://www.apress.com.

The information in this book is distributed on an "as is" basis, without warranty. Although every precaution has been taken in the preparation of this work, neither the author(s) nor Apress shall have any liability to any person or entity with respect to any loss or damage caused or alleged to be caused directly or indirectly by the information contained in this work.

The source code for this book is available to readers at http://www.apress.com in the Source Code section.

Contents at a Glance

Contents

About the Author

DEBRA DALGLEISH is a computer consultant in Mississauga, Ontario, Canada, serving local and international clients. Self-employed since 1985, she has extensive experience in designing complex Excel and Access applications, as well as sophisticated Word forms and documents. She has led hundreds of Microsoft Office corporate training sessions, from beginner to advanced level.

In recognition of her contributions to the Excel newsgroups, she has received the Microsoft Office Excel MVP award each year since 2001. You can find a wide variety of Excel tips and tutorials, and sample files, on her Contextures website: `www.contextures.com/tiptech.html`.

About the Technical Reviewer

DON REAMEY is a Software Development Engineer for Microsoft's Office Business Applications Group, where he works on applications that integrate line-of-business systems with Microsoft Office. Don has 16 years of experience in the software industry, with 10 of those years building C++ and Java applications for the financial industry. Don holds a bachelor of science degree in information systems from Pfeiffer University.

Acknowledgments

Many people helped me as I worked on this book. Above all, love and thanks to Keith, who has believed in me from the start and provided endless encouragement, and to Jason, Sarah, and Neven, for enduring months of stress. (It's safe to come home now!)

Thanks to Andy Pope for introducing me to the wonderful people at Apress: Dominic Shakeshaft, who helped develop the book's concept; Ewan Buckingham, who created a structure for the book's material; and Kylie Johnston, who kept everything on track. Thanks also to Don Reamey, for his insightful questions during the technical review; Liz Welch, who polished the text and ensured it was consistent; and my vigilant production editor, Katie Stence.

Many thanks to Dave Peterson, from whom I've learned much about Excel programming, and who graciously commented on some of the code for this book. Thanks to Jon Peltier, who convinced me to start writing about pivot tables, and who is always willing to exchange ideas and humor, and to Tom Ogilvy, who generously shares his creative code. Thanks to all those who ask questions and provide answers in the Microsoft Excel newsgroups, and were the inspiration for many of the recipes in this book.

Thanks to my clients, who remained patient as I juggled projects and writing, and who continue to challenge me with interesting assignments.

Finally, thanks to my parents, Doug and Shirley McConnell, and my sister Nancy Nelson, for a lifetime of love and support.

Introduction

Excel's pivot tables are a powerful tool for analyzing data. With only a few minutes of work, a new user can create an attractively formatted table that summarizes thousands of rows of data. This book assumes that you know the basics of Excel and pivot tables, and provides troubleshooting tips and techniques, as well as programming examples.

Who This Book Is For

This book is for anyone who uses pivot tables, and who reads the manual only when all else fails. It's designed to help you understand the advanced features and options that are available, as you need them. Experiment with pivot tables, and if you get stuck, search for the problem in this book. With luck, you'll find a solution, a workaround, or, occasionally, confirmation that pivot tables can't do what you want them to do.

How This Book Is Structured

Chapters 1 to 12 contain manual solutions to common pivot table problems, and alert you to the situations where no known solution exists. Chapter 13 has sample code for those who prefer a programming solution to their pivot table problems. The following is a brief summary of the material contained in each chapter.

- Chapter 1, "Creating a Pivot Table": Topics include issues you should consider when planning a pivot table and preparing the source data; problems that occur when connecting to the source data; and understanding the pivot table options that are available.

- Chapter 2, "Sorting and Grouping Pivot Table Data": You'll learn how data sorts in a pivot table, as well as how to create custom sort orders, show top items only, and group and ungroup numbers, dates, and text.

- Chapter 3, "Calculations in a Pivot Table": This chapter discusses using the summary functions and custom calculations, creating calculated items and calculated fields to expand the built-in capabilities, modifying formulas, and adjusting the solve order.

- Chapter 4, "Formatting a Pivot Table": You'll learn about autoformatting a pivot table, applying and retaining formatting, creating custom number formats, and showing and hiding totals and subtotals.

- Chapter 5, "Extracting Pivot Table Data": Topics include using the Drill to Details feature to extract underlying records, using the GetPivotData worksheet function to return pivot table data, turning off the GetPivotData feature, and creating pivot table copies with the Show Pages feature.

- Chapter 6, "Modifying a Pivot Table": This chapter covers changing the pivot table layout, modifying field and item captions, clearing old items from the field drop-downs, adding comments to data cells, and customizing the PivotTable toolbar.

- Chapter 7, "Updating a Pivot Table": Topics include refreshing the pivot table, refreshing automatically, reconnecting to the source data, changing the source data, and creating a dynamic source data range.

- Chapter 8, "Securing a Pivot Table": This chapter discusses preventing users from changing the pivot table layout, connecting to a password-protected data source, using security features, and addressing privacy issues.

- Chapter 9, "Pivot Table Limits and Performance": This chapter covers understanding limits to pivot table field size, addressing memory issues, maximizing performance, and reducing file size.

- Chapter 10, "Publishing a Pivot Table": This chapter explains how to prepare a pivot table for publishing on a web page, with or without interactivity.

- Chapter 11, "Printing a Pivot Table": Topics include printing headings on every page, repeating row and column labels, adjusting the print area, and using the Report Manager to simplify printing.

- Chapter 12, "Pivot Charts": This chapter covers restoring lost formatting, creating normal charts from pivot tables, stepping through the Chart Wizard when creating a pivot chart, and modifying a pivot chart layout.

- Chapter 13, "Programming a Pivot Table": You'll learn how to record and use macros, and edit recorded code. This chapter includes sample code for modifying and printing pivot tables and clearing old items from pivot field dropdown lists, and it discusses refreshing pivot tables on protected sheets, preventing layout changes, reformatting a pivot chart, and changing the pivot cache.

Prerequisites

The solutions in this book are written for Microsoft Excel 2003. Most will work in Excel 2002, but may not adapt to earlier versions. A working knowledge of Excel is assumed, as well as familiarity with pivot table basics. Sample code is provided in Chapter 13, and some programming experience may be required to adjust the code to conform to your workbook setup.

For an introduction to pivot tables, see *A Complete Guide to PivotTables: A Visual Approach*, by Paul Cornell (Apress, 2005).

Downloading the Code

Sample workbooks and code are available for download from the Apress website.

Contacting the Author

The author can be contacted at ddalgleish@contextures.com. Visit her Contextures website at www.contextures.com.

■ ■ ■

CHAPTER 1

Creating a Pivot Table

Even though you've likely created many PivotTable reports in Microsoft Excel, you sometimes encounter problems while setting them up. Perhaps the layout isn't as flexible as you'd like, or you have trouble connecting to the data source that you want to use. The PivotTable and PivotChart Wizard provides many options as you create the PivotTable report, and you want to understand the effect the different settings have. This chapter discusses the issues you can consider as you plan the PivotTable report, set up the source data, connect to the source, and select the PivotTable options.

1.1. Planning a Pivot Table: Getting Started

Problem

You've been asked to create a pivot table from your company's sales data, and you aren't sure what issues to consider before you create it.

Solution

If you spend some time planning, you can create a pivot table that is easier to maintain and that clearly delivers the information your customers need. When planning a pivot table, you should consider several things:

- What type of data is available as the source for the pivot table?

- Where is the source data stored?

- Will you need to share this information with others?

1.2. Planning a Pivot Table: Accessing the Source Data

Problem

You've been asked to create a pivot table from your company's sales data, and you need to determine what type of source data you'll use.

Solution

In the first step of the PivotTable and PivotChart Wizard, you select a data source for your pivot table from the list of four source types:

- Microsoft Excel list or database

- External data source

- Multiple consolidation ranges

- Another PivotTable report or PivotChart report

Many pivot tables are created from a single Excel list, usually in the same workbook as the pivot table. Others are created from multiple Excel lists, or another source, such as a database query, online analytical processing (OLAP) cube, or an existing pivot table in the same workbook.

To determine if the source data can be used in its current state, here are some things to consider.

Where Is the Raw Data Stored?

To create a meaningful pivot table, you need current, accurate data. Is the raw data in your workbook updated by you on a regular basis? Or is the raw data stored elsewhere?

If others are using the pivot table, and the data is not stored in the workbook, will they have access to the source data when they want to refresh the pivot table?

How Frequently Will the Raw Data Be Updated?

If the raw data will be updated frequently, you may want a routine that automatically refreshes the pivot table when the workbook is opened. If the data is stored outside of the workbook, how will you be notified that the data has changed and that you need to refresh the pivot table?

What Problems Might You, or Other Users, Have in Accessing the Raw Data?

Does every user have access to the source data? Should there be a routine to refresh the pivot table on a regular basis?

If the source data is password protected, will all users know the password?

1.3. Planning a Pivot Table: Source Data Fields

Problem

You've been asked to create a pivot table from your company's sales data, and you need to know if the source data has all the fields you need to create your report.

Solution

The source data may contain all the fields that you want in the pivot table. However, you may need to report on other fields. For example, if variance from plan to budget is required in the pivot table, is variance a field in the source data? If not, you'll need some way to calculate that in the pivot table, or add it to the fields in the source data.

If fields are missing from the source data, can they be calculated at the source, or will they be calculated in the pivot table? What is the effect of either option?

1.4. Planning a Shared Pivot Table

Problem

You've been asked to create a pivot table from your company's sales data, and make the results available to other employees.

Solution

If a pivot table will be shared with others, here are some things to consider.

Will All Users Need the Same Level of Detail?

Some users may require a top-level summary of the data. For example, the senior executives may want to see a total per region for annual sales. Other users may require greater detail. The regional directors may want to see the data totaled by district, or by sales representative. Sales representatives may need the data totaled by customer, or by product number.

If the requirements are varied, you may want to create multiple pivot tables, each one focused on the needs of a particular user group. If that's not possible, you'll want to create a pivot table that's easy to navigate, and adaptable for each user group's needs.

Is the Information Sensitive?

Often, a pivot table is based on sensitive data. For example, the source data may contain sales results and commission figures for all the sales representatives. If you create a pivot table from the data, assume that anyone who can open the workbook will be able to view all the data. Even if you protect the worksheet, and the workbook, the data won't be secure. Some passwords can be easily cracked, allowing the protection to be bypassed. This weakness is described in Excel's Help files, under the heading, "About worksheet and workbook protection." It includes the warning, "With enough time, users can obtain and modify all the data in a workbook, as long as they have access to it."

When requiring a password to open the workbook, use a strong password, as described in the Microsoft article "Implementing Guidelines for Strong Passwords," at `www.microsoft.com/ntserver/techresources/security/password.asp`.

■**Note** A strong password contains a mixture of upper- and lowercase letters, numbers, and special characters (such as $ and %), and is at least six characters long.

For sensitive and confidential data, the pivot table should only be based on the data that each user is entitled to view. You can create multiple source lists, in separate workbooks, and create individual pivot tables from those. It will require more time to set these up, but it will be worthwhile to ensure that privacy concerns are addressed. You can use macros and naming conventions to standardize the source data and the pivot tables, and to minimize the work required to create the individual copies.

Another option is to use secured network folders to store the workbook, where only authorized users can access the data. Also available in Excel 2003 is Information Rights Management, a file-protection technology that allows you to assign permissions to users or groups. For example, some users can have Read permission only, and won't be able to edit, copy, or print the file contents. Other users, with Change permission, can edit and save changes. You can also set expiry dates for the permissions to limit access to a specific time period. To learn more about Information Rights Management, see Excel's Help files, and check out "Information Rights Management in Office Professional Edition 2003" at `www.microsoft.com/office/editions/prodinfo/technologies/irm.mspx`. The Microsoft Office 2003 Security Whitepaper discusses the security technologies available in Excel, as well as other Office programs, at `www.microsoft.com/technet/prodtechnol/office/office2003/operate/o3secdet.mspx#EEAA`.

Will the Information Be Shared in Printed or Electronic Format?

If the information will be shared in printed format only, the security issues are minimized. You can control what's printed and issued to each recipient. If the information will be shared electronically, it's crucial that confidential data not be included in any pivot table that's being distributed to multiple users.

Will the Pivot Table Be in a Shared Workbook?

Many features are unavailable in a shared workbook, including creating or changing a PivotTable report or chart. Users will be able to view your pivot table, but won't be able to rearrange the fields or select different items from the dropdown lists.

Also, protection can't be changed in a shared workbook, so you can't run macros that unprotect the worksheet, make changes, and then reprotect the worksheet.

Will Users Enable Macros in Your Workbook?

If your pivot table requires macros for some functionality, will users have the ability to enable macros? In some environments, they may not be able to use macros. Will that have a serious impact on the value of your pivot table?

1.5. Preparing the Source Data: Using an Excel List

Problem

You want to create a pivot table from an Excel list. Before starting the PivotTable and PivotChart Wizard, you want to ensure that your database is in the required format.

Solution

Probably the most common data source for a pivot table is an Excel list, in the same workbook as the pivot table. The list may contain only a few rows of records, or it may contain thousands of records. No matter what size the list is, there are common requirements when preparing to base a pivot table on the data.

How Should Your List Be Arranged in Order to Create a Pivot Table?

- Your list should have a heading in each cell in the first row.

- There should be no blank rows or columns within the list.

Tip Select a cell in the list, then while holding down the Ctrl key, press the asterisk key (*) to select the current region. If the complete list isn't selected, there are probably blank rows or columns within the list. Locate and delete them, or enter data in them.

- Each column should contain the same type of data. For example, one column may contain sales amounts in currency. Another column may contain region names in text. Another column may contain order dates.

- If you plan to group the data in the pivot table, ensure that each row contains data in the fields you want to group. For example, enter an order date in each row.

Tip If no date is available, you could create a dummy date for use in those rows. Make the dummy date obvious, so it won't be confused with real data.

- Remove any total calculations at the top or bottom of the list, as well as any manually entered subtotals within the list.

- Name the range so you can refer to that name when creating the pivot table.

- If the list will grow or shrink, use a dynamic name for the range.

- If the Subtotals feature is turned on in the list, remove the subtotals. Otherwise, the PivotTable and PivotChart Wizard will prevent you from creating the pivot table.

- If the AutoFilter feature is turned on, you can leave it on. It won't have any effect on creating the pivot table, and the pivot table will be based on all data, whether it's hidden or visible.

- If rows or columns have been manually hidden, you can leave them hidden. They won't have any effect on creating the pivot table, and the pivot table will be based on all rows and columns, whether they're hidden or visible.

Tip If columns are hidden, check that they contain data in the heading cells, or you won't be able to create a pivot table from the list.

1.6. Preparing the Source Data: Excel List Invalid Field Names

Problem

You want to create a pivot table from an Excel list, but you get an error message about invalid field names.

Solution

One or more of the heading cells in the Excel list may be blank, and to create a pivot table you need a heading for each column. In Step 2 of the PivotTable and PivotChart Wizard, check carefully to ensure that you haven't selected extra columns. Also, check that there aren't hidden columns within the source data range, as they may have blank heading cells.

1.7. Preparing the Source Data: Using a Filtered Excel List

Problem

You want to create a pivot table from a filtered Excel list, but all the records are included when you create the pivot table, instead of just the filtered items.

Solution

A pivot table includes all the items from the source list, even if the list has an AutoFilter or Advanced Filter applied, hiding some of the rows. Instead of filtering the list in place, you could use an Advanced Filter to extract some records to another worksheet, and then base the pivot table on the extracted list.

1.8. Preparing the Source Data: Using an Excel List with Monthly Columns

Problem

Your Excel list has a column for each month, and you're having trouble creating a flexible pivot table from this source data. Each month gets its own field button, and it's difficult to get the layout you want in the pivot table, and to create annual totals.

Solution

In your Excel list, the column headings contain Pivot Field Item names, instead of Pivot Field names. For example, instead of a column heading Month, each month has its own heading, and the data for that month is entered there. This is a great way to create a summary report in your workbook but isn't ideal for creating a pivot table. If you create a pivot table from the Excel list, you'll need 12 data fields, one for each month, and will need another field to total the monthly data.

You should rearrange the data, using actual dates, if available, or month names, in a single column, with the sales amounts all in one column. Instead of 13 columns (Product and one for each of the 12 months), the revised list will have three columns: Product, Month, and Amount. This will normalize the data and allow a more flexible pivot table to be created.

For information on normalization, you can read the Microsoft Knowledge Base article "Description of the Database Normalization Basics" at http://support.microsoft.com/kb/283878. The following technique will automate the normalization process for you. It creates a pivot table from the existing list, and combines all the Month columns into one field. Then, the Drill to Details feature is used to extract the source data in its one-column format.

Tip If you have data for each item, for each month, you'll increase the required rows 12-fold, so check that you won't exceed Excel's row limit before trying the following technique. If your normalized data will exceed Excel's row limit, you could process the columns in two or more sessions, and store the data in an external database.

Assuming you have a simple list, with one column of product names, and 12 columns of monthly sales figures, follow these steps:

1. Select a cell in the list.

2. Choose Data ➤ PivotTable and PivotChart Report.

3. In Step 1, select Multiple Consolidation Ranges, select PivotTable as the type of report, and then click Next.

4. In Step 2a, select the I will create the page fields option, then click Next.

5. In Step 2b, select your list on the worksheet, then click the Add button.

6. Leave the other settings at their defaults, and click the Next button.

Tip The next step isn't required, but will create a much smaller pivot table, in which only the Grand Total is visible in the data area.

7. In Step 3, click the Layout button, and in the Layout window, drag the Row and Column field buttons off the pivot table, leaving only the Sum of Value field in the data area. Then click OK.

8. Click Finish, and a pivot table appears in the workbook, with a PivotTable Field List that contains only three fields: Row, Column, and Value.

9. In the pivot table that was created, double-click on the Grand Total cell to drill down and create a list of underlying data.

Tip You can use an AutoFilter to remove the rows with blank value cells. To filter the list, choose Data ➤ Filter ➤ AutoFilter. From the dropdown list in the Value column, choose Blanks. Delete the filtered rows, then choose Data ➤ Filter ➤ AutoFilter to remove the AutoFilter.

10. In the resulting list of data, rename the heading cells as Product, Month, and Amount.

Tip This normalized list will be used as the source for your new pivot table. Make a backup copy of the file, then you can delete the original list and its pivot table. You can also delete the sheet that contains the pivot table used in Step 10.

11. Create a pivot table from the normalized list, with Product in the row area, Month in the column area, and Amount in the data area. Because there's only one data field, the Row Grand Total will automatically sum the Months. In the old version of the pivot table, with 12 month fields, you had to create a calculated field to sum the months.

1.9. Preparing the Source Data: Using an Excel List with Monthly Columns and Text Fields

Problem

You'd like to use the normalization technique described in Section 1.8, but you have two columns with text, then your columns of monthly data. The normalization technique only works with one column of text data.

Solution

If you have two or more text columns, you should concatenate them before using the normalization technique. For example, if you have columns for Name and Region, follow these steps:

1. Insert a blank column after Region, with the heading NameRegion.

2. In cell C2, enter the formula

   ```
   =A2 & "$" & B2
   ```

3. Copy the formula down to the last row of data.

4. Follow steps 1 to 10 in the normalization instructions from Section 1.8, using columns C:O as the source range for the pivot table.

5. In the resulting list of data, rename the heading cells as NameRegion, Month, and Amount.

6. Select column A (NameRegion), and move it to the right of the other columns. This will prevent it from overwriting the other columns when you separate Name and Region in the next step.

7. With the NameRegion column selected, choose Data ➤ Text to Columns.

8. Select Delimited, and click the Next button.

9. Select the Other option, and in the text box, type the $ sign.

10. Click Finish to split the text into two columns.

11. Add headings to the columns, and rearrange them, if desired.

12. Create a pivot table from the normalized list, with Name and Region in the row area, Month in the column area, and Amount in the data area.

1.10. Preparing the Source Data: Using an Access Query

Problem

You want to create a pivot table from a Microsoft Access query, but you aren't sure what fields to include in the query.

Solution

In the Access query, include all the fields that you want in the pivot table. If you use lookup tables, include them in the query, and add the descriptive field names to the query output instead of using ID numbers or codes. For example, an OrderDetail table might include a product number. Another table (Products) in the database contains the information about each product number, such as the product name and color. In the query, add both tables, then join the Product number field in the two tables. In the query grid, include fields from the OrderDetail table, such as Quantity, and from the Products table, include descriptive fields, such as Product Name and Color.

Also, in the Access query create calculated fields for any line calculations you want summarized in the pivot table, such as LineTotal:UnitsSold*UnitPrice.

■**Caution** Although they're permissible within Microsoft Access, user-defined functions, and some built-in Access functions such as NZ, will create an error, for example, "Undefined function 'NZ' in expression," when used outside of Access. For more information on the Jet SQL expressions that are used to return the data to Excel, see "Microsoft Jet SQL Reference" at `http://office.microsoft.com/en-ca/assistance/` `CH062526881033.aspx`. For more information on Access queries, see "Queries" at `http://office.` `microsoft.com/en-us/assistance/CH062526491033.aspx`.

1.11. Preparing the Source Data: Using an Access Query with Parameters

Problem

You want to base your pivot table on a Microsoft Access query that contains parameters, but you get an error message saying you can't use parameters.

Solution

In Access, you can use parameters in the criteria row of a query, and you are prompted to enter the criteria when the query runs. However, you can't create a pivot table that's directly based on a parameter query. Instead, you can use page fields to filter the pivot table:

1. In Access, create a query without parameters.

2. In Excel, create a pivot table based on the query without parameters.

3. Place the field that you want to filter in the pivot table's page area.

4. Select an item from the page field, and the pivot table will display the data for that item only.

1.12. Preparing the Source Data: Using a Text File

Problem

The accounting department can provide you with a text file of the year-to-date transactions, which you can use as a data source for your pivot table. They've asked how you want the file set up.

Solution

You can use a delimited or fixed-width text file as the data source for a pivot file, but it's usually easier to work with a delimited file. It requires only one setting to separate the fields. If using a fixed-width file, you have to specify the start position and length of each field.

If possible, include field headings in the first row, and ensure that there is a line break character at the end of each record.

1.13. Preparing the Source Data: Using an OLAP Cube

Problem

You want to base your pivot table on an OLAP cube that you'll create from data in your Access database. You aren't sure what should be included in the Access query that will provide the source data for the cube.

Solution

An online analytical processing (OLAP) database, also referred to as an OLAP cube, is a way of organizing a large amount of data. It organizes the database fields in levels and makes it more efficient for you to work with the data. For example, Date fields can be organized into levels such as Month, Quarter, and Year. A related set of levels is called a dimension. The data for each dimension is summarized, and can be used in your pivot table.

Each field can be used only once in the OLAP cube, so if you'll need a field twice—for example, an Average and a Sum—you'll need two copies of the field in the Access query.

Include at least one field that is a measure (data to be summarized), and other fields that you can use in the row, column, or page area.

1.14. Preparing the Source Data: Creating an OLAP Cube

Problem

You want to base your pivot table on an OLAP cube, but you don't know how to create one.

Solution

In the PivotTable and PivotChart Wizard, if you select the External data source option in Step 1, you'll have the opportunity to create an OLAP cube from your data source in the final step of the Query Wizard or in Microsoft Query. The OLAP Cube Wizard will guide you through the process.

1.15. Preparing the Source Data: Using Multiple Consolidation Ranges

Problem

You have an Excel list with each region's sales on separate sheets in your workbook, and want to combine all the data into one pivot table. You created a pivot table and selected the Multiple consolidation ranges option in Step 1 of the PivotTable and PivotChart Wizard, but the pivot table doesn't look like your other pivot tables, and you can't get it to work correctly.

Solution

Creating a pivot table from multiple consolidation ranges allows you to create a pivot table from data in two or more separate lists. However, the result is not the same as a pivot table created from a single Excel list. The first field is placed in the row area, the remaining field names are placed in the column area, and the values in those columns appear in the data area.

You can hide or show the column items, and use the page fields to filter the data. However, there's no setting you can change to create a pivot table from multiple consolidation ranges that's a different structure than the standard result.

1.16. Preparing the Source Data: Alternatives to Using Multiple Consolidation Ranges

Problem

The results aren't satisfactory when you create a pivot table from multiple consolidation ranges. What are the alternatives?

Solution

Instead of using multiple consolidation ranges, you may be able to cut and paste all the data onto one worksheet. If there are too many rows to fit on one Excel worksheet, consider storing the data in a database, and create a pivot table from the external source.

1.17. Preparing the Source Data: Setting Up Multiple Consolidation Ranges

Problem

You have too much data to store on one worksheet, you have no control over the source data, or you are unable to move the data to a database. You can't use one of the alternatives, and have to create a pivot table from multiple consolidation ranges. What's the best way to set up a pivot table from multiple consolidation ranges?

Solution

First, ensure that all the ranges being used are identical in setup. Each list should have the same column headings, in the same order, and contain the same type of data. The ranges can contain different numbers of rows.

The first column will be used as a row heading in the pivot table, so move the most important field to that position.

1.18. Preparing the Source Data: Benefits of Using Another PivotTable or PivotChart Report

Problem

You have to create a new pivot table from the same source as an existing pivot table. What are the benefits of basing a pivot table on another pivot table?

Solution

When you create a pivot table, Excel stores a copy of the source data in a memory area called a pivot cache. If you base a pivot table on another pivot table, it uses the same pivot cache as the first pivot table. This may result in a smaller file size, and less memory used in Excel. To view the memory used, you can check the list of processes in the Windows Task Manager, or, in Excel, enter the following formula on a worksheet:

```
=INFO("MemUsed")
```

This returns the number of bytes of memory being used for data.

1.19. Preparing the Source Data: Problems Caused by Using Another PivotTable or PivotChart Report

Problem

You have to create a new pivot table from the same source as an existing pivot table. What problems might you encounter if you base the new pivot table on the existing pivot table?

Solution

If you group fields in one pivot table, those fields are also grouped in the other pivot table. This might cause unexpected layout changes in a pivot table.

You won't be able to refresh the pivot tables separately; if you refresh either pivot table, the other pivot table will automatically be refreshed.

1.20. Preparing the Source Data: Page Field Settings When Using Another PivotTable or PivotChart Report

Problem

You have to create a new pivot table from the same source as an existing pivot table in the same workbook. In Step 1 of the PivotTable and PivotChart Wizard, the option to use another PivotTable or PivotChart report is not available.

Solution

If you've set the page fields in a PivotTable to the Query external data source as you select each field option, you won't be able to use the pivot table as a source for your new pivot table. If the pivot table is the only one in the active workbook, the Another PivotTable report or PivotChart report option will be disabled in the list of data sources (see Figure 1-1).

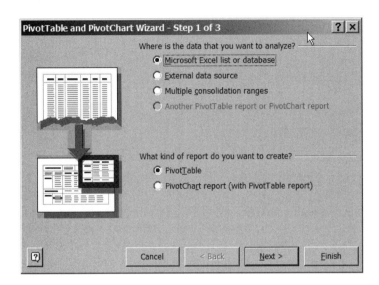

Figure 1-1. *The PivotTable option is disabled in the PivotTable and PivotChart Wizard.*

To change the setting, double-click each page field in the source pivot table, and click the Advanced button.

Set the Page field options to Retrieve external data for all page field items.

1.21. Connecting to the Source Data: Selecting a Large Range in an Excel List

Problem

How can you select a large list easily when you're setting the source range in the PivotTable and PivotChart Wizard?

Solution

While in the PivotTable and PivotChart Wizard, you can use the keyboard to select the range. For example, press Ctrl+Home to select the first cell on the worksheet.

■**Note** If Freeze Panes have been applied, the Ctrl+Home shortcut will activate the first cell in the unfrozen part of the window.

After you've selected the starting cell, press the Shift key. This will expand the selection as you use the navigation keys.

To select cells to the right of the active cell, press the End key, then press the Right arrow key. To select cells below the active cell, press the End key, then press the Down arrow key.

For example, to select a list that starts at the top left of the worksheet, follow these steps:

1. Press Ctrl+Home, to go to the top left of the worksheet.

2. Hold the Shift key, and press and release the End key, then the Right arrow key.

3. Hold the Shift key, and press and release the End key, then the Down arrow key.

1.22. Connecting to the Source Data: Using Arrow Keys in an Excel List

Problem

While selecting a worksheet range in the PivotTable and PivotChart Wizard, you aren't able to use the arrow keys.

Solution

Whether or not the arrow keys work depends on how you open the wizard. If you right-click on the PivotTable and choose PivotTable Wizard, the arrow keys won't work. However, if you click the PivotTable button on the Pivot toolbar and choose PivotTable Wizard, or open the wizard from the Data menu, the shortcut keys will work when selecting the range.

1.23. Connecting to the Source Data: Installing Drivers for External Data

Problem

You want to base your pivot table on an external source, but you don't know what drivers you need installed.

Solution

To connect to external data, Microsoft Query must be installed on your machine, as well as the appropriate Open Database Connectivity (ODBC) drivers or data source drivers. Microsoft Office includes drivers for the following data sources:

- Microsoft Excel

- Microsoft Access

- Microsoft SQL Server OLAP Services

- SQL Server

- Text file databases

- dBASE

- Microsoft FoxPro

- Oracle

- Paradox

- Third-party providers

These drivers are installed when you install Excel. If your external data source isn't supported by one of these ODBC drivers, you may be able to obtain a Microsoft Office–compatible ODBC driver, along with installation instructions, from the database vendor.

1.24. Connecting to the Source Data: Creating a New Source for External Data

Problem

In Step 2 of the PivotTable and PivotChart Wizard, you clicked the Get Data button to open the Choose Data Source dialog box. You want to connect to an external data source that isn't listed.

Solution

In the Choose Data Source dialog box, both the OLAP cubes tab and the Database tab have a New Data Source option, which allows you to create additional data sources. You can save additional queries later in the dialog box, and they'll be added to the Queries tab.

■**Tip** If you select an OLAP cube, then try to change it to a different data source, you'll receive an error message. You can cancel out of the PivotTable and PivotChart Wizard, and restart.

To create a new data source in the Choose Data Source dialog box, follow these steps:

1. On the Database tab, select New Data Source, and click the OK button.

2. In the Create New Data Source dialog box, type a name for the data source.

3. In box 2, select a driver for the type of database that you will use as your data source.

4. Click the Connect button.

5. The next step will vary, depending on which driver you selected. For example, if you selected an Access driver, the ODBC Microsoft Access Setup dialog box appears, where you can click the Select button and select the database to which you want to connect. To change some of the settings, click the Advanced button, select an option in the list, and change its value.

■Note If using a text file to create the data source, you may see an error message, advising you that the INI file is corrupted. This can be resolved by obtaining a hotfix from Microsoft, as described in the following Microsoft Knowledge Base article: `http://support.microsoft.com/kb/884038`.

---

6. Click OK to return to the Create New Data Source dialog box.

7. In box 4, you can select a table as the default.

8. At the bottom of the dialog box, you can add a checkmark to store your user ID and password in the DSN file. This may compromise your database security, and you may prefer to manually enter this information when connecting to the database.

9. Click OK to return to the Choose Data Source dialog box.

1.25. Connecting to the Source Data: Excel Hangs When Using External Data

Problem

Excel hangs when you try to create a PivotTable from an external data source.

Solution

Microsoft Query may be open in the background, waiting for you to respond.

1. Click the Microsoft Query button on the Windows Taskbar to activate the program.

2. In Microsoft Query, click the Return Data button.

This should close Microsoft Query, and allow you to continue working in Excel.

1.26. Connecting to the Source Data: Using Pages with Multiple Consolidation Ranges

Problem

You have each salesperson's orders listed on a separate worksheet, and you're creating a pivot table from all the data. When you create a pivot table from multiple consolidation ranges, you have the option to create page fields, but you aren't sure how they work.

Solution

In the PivotTable and PivotChart Wizard, after you select Multiple Consolidation Ranges as the data source, Step 2a asks, "How many page fields do you want?" You can let Excel create one page field, or you can create the page fields yourself.

Create a Single Page Field for Me

If you select this option, one page field is created automatically. In Step 2b of the Pivot-Table and PivotChart Wizard, you aren't presented with any options for creating the page fields. In the completed pivot table, there's one page field, and each range in the multiple consolidation ranges is represented as a numbered item—for example, Item1, Item2, and Item3.

This makes it difficult to determine which data you're viewing when you select one of the items from the dropdown list. However, if you're more interested in the total amounts than in the individual ranges, this is a quick way to create the page field.

I Will Create the Page Fields

If you select this option, you can create the page fields in Step 2b of the PivotTable and PivotChart Wizard. To create the page fields, follow these steps:

1. In Step 2b, select each range, and add it to the All ranges list.

2. Select the number of page fields that you want to create (zero to four). In this example, there will be two page fields.

3. In the All ranges list, select the first range.

4. You'll use the first page field to show the salesperson names. In the dropdown list for Field one, type the name of the person whose range you have highlighted in the list.

5. Each salesperson works in one of your sales regions, and you'll use the second page field to show the Region names. In the dropdown list for Field two, type the region name for the person whose range you have highlighted in the list, as shown in Figure 1-2.

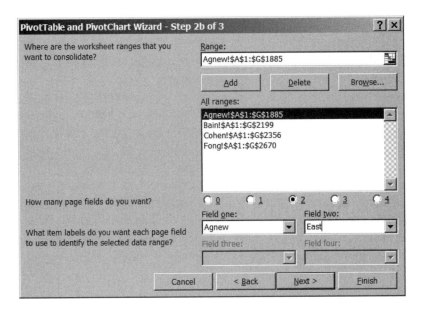

Figure 1-2. *Create page fields for multiple consolidation ranges.*

6. Select the next range in the All ranges list, and repeat Steps 4 and 5. Continue until all the ranges have page labels.

■Tip After you have created a label, you can select that label from the dropdown list for subsequent entries.

---

7. Click Next, then click Finish to close the PivotTable and PivotChart Wizard.

8. In the pivot table, the page fields that you created have numbered buttons, Page1 and Page2. You can change the button labels by typing over them. Select the cell that has the Page1 button, and type **Salesperson**, then select the cell that has the Page2 button, and type **Region**.

1.27. Understanding PivotTable Options: Table Name

Problem

Excel names your pivot tables with meaningless names like PivotTable1. You'd like to name the pivot table when you're creating it.

Solution

In the last step of the PivotTable and PivotChart Wizard, click the Options button to set general options for the pivot table that you're creating. At the top of the PivotTable Options dialog box is the Name box. You can refer to this to see the name that was automatically assigned when the pivot table was created. You can change the name to something more meaningful—for example, Sales Pivot instead of PivotTable1.

1.28. Understanding PivotTable Options: Table Naming Rules

Problem

What are the rules for naming a pivot table?

Solution

Although the naming rules for other items, such as macros or worksheets, are somewhat strict, the rules for naming pivot tables are quite flexible. For example, a worksheet name is limited to a maximum of 31 characters, and can't include characters such as a question mark or colon. However, a pivot table name can include these characters, or the name could even be a single space character.

Warning While you can include these characters in a pivot table name, I suggest you avoid them, as well as other characters such as slashes, square brackets, and asterisks, as they might cause problems when you're programming.

1.29. Understanding PivotTable Options: Row and Column Grand Totals

Problem

Sometimes Row and Column Grand Totals appear and sometimes they don't. What controls them?

Solution

For pivot tables, Row and Column Grand Totals are turned on by default. If you have at least one field in the row area, the Column Grand Totals will appear. If you have at least one field in the column area, the Row Grand Totals will appear.

In some pivot tables, these totals are meaningless and should be turned off. In other pivot tables, you can leave them on, or turn them off to simplify the layout.

To turn them off, in the last step of the PivotTable and PivotChart Wizard, click the Options button and remove the checkmark from Row Grand Totals and/or Column Grand Totals.

1.30. Understanding PivotTable Options: AutoFormat Table

Problem

What does the AutoFormat Table option do? Even when it's off, the pivot table seems to format itself.

Solution

If the AutoFormat Table option is on, the default PivotTable format will be applied to your pivot table. You can turn this feature off, or apply other AutoFormats to the pivot table, by choosing Format ➤ AutoFormat.

However, you may find that the formatting is very persistent. You can turn off the AutoFormat option, format the pivot table with no borders or fill color, but when you refresh the pivot table or rearrange the layout, some of the cell borders and fill color will return.

If you want the column widths to remain a specific size, turn off the AutoFormat option. Otherwise, when you select a different item from the page field dropdown lists, the column widths will change to match the width of the selected item.

1.31. Understanding PivotTable Options: Subtotal Hidden Page Items

Problem

What does the Subtotal hidden page items option do?

Solution

You can hide page items by double-clicking on the page field button and selecting items in the Hide items list. Normally, these items are not included in the pivot table subtotals or grand totals. When you turn on the Subtotal hidden page items option, the items are included.

Also, when page items are hidden, and you select the (All) item from the dropdown list, the cell displays (Multiple Items). If Subtotal hidden page items is on, the cell displays (All).

■**Note** This option is not available for OLAP-based pivot tables.

1.32. Understanding PivotTable Options: Merge Labels

Problem

Is there any benefit to using the Merge Labels option?

Solution

If this option is turned on, cells for the outer level row and column heading labels are merged. Normally, if you select a cell in the label area, only that cell is selected, indicating that the cells are not merged. If you turn on the Merge labels option, and select a cell in the label area, the entire range of cells is selected, indicating that the cells are merged. Changing this option is the only way to merge the cells in a pivot table. You can't manually select and merge, or unmerge, them.

Note All outer fields are affected—you can't apply this setting to specific fields.

The most common reason for using this feature is to have the outer field labels centered vertically. However, a side effect of turning this option on is that the merged labels, along with the related subtotals, are vertically and horizontally centered instead of left and bottom aligned.

1.33. Understanding PivotTable Options: Merge Labels Formatting

Problem

If you try to change the cell alignment of an outer field or its subtotal label when the Merge labels option is on, you'll receive an error message (see Figure 1-3).

Figure 1-3. *Error message that appears when you try to format a merged label*

Solution

To overcome this limitation, you can select a cell, click the Increase Indent button on the Formatting toolbar, then click the Decrease Indent button on the Formatting toolbar. This will change the cell's alignment to left aligned.

Note Other alignment options, such as right aligned or rotated text, are not available for outer field labels and their subtotals when the Merge labels option is on.

1.34. Understanding PivotTable Options: Preserve Formatting

Problem

When you refresh the pivot table, formatting that you've applied is removed.

Solution

If the Preserve Formatting option is on, you can apply formatting to cells in the pivot table, and it should be retained when the pivot table is refreshed or the layout changed.

1.35. Understanding PivotTable Options: Repeat Item Labels on Each Printed Page

Problem

You have created a large pivot table, and when you print it, the column and row headings don't print on each page when a field is continued on subsequent pages.

Solution

You can turn on the Repeat item labels on each printed page option if you're printing a large pivot table, and the outer headings are continued on multiple pages. For example, with the row fields Region, SalesRep, and Product, the rows for a large region may fill more than one page. If this option is not on, the Region name would print with its first SalesRep name. On the second, and subsequent pages, the Region name wouldn't appear.

However, if the option is on, the relevant Region name would appear at the top of each page of the printed pivot table.

■**Note** If the Merge labels option is on, the Repeat item labels on each printed page option has no effect. Row item labels are printed only once, near the center of the merged field label.

1.36. Understanding PivotTable Options: Page Layout

Problem

You have several page fields, and they use a great deal of space at the top of the work-sheet, which makes it harder to work with your pivot table.

Solution

The Page layout option, in conjunction with the Fields per Column/Row option, allows you to make better use of this space. Instead of one tall column of page fields, you can have multiple, smaller stacks. The Page layout option controls how the page fields are placed in the multiple stacks, and provides two choices: Down, then Over, or Over, then Down.

Tip With either option, the new arrangement will have the same ending row as the original page area. You can delete rows above the new page area to reduce the amount of space at the top of the worksheet.

How It Works

Let's look at the two options for Page layout.

Down, then Over

When Down, then Over is selected, the option that follows is Fields per column. In the Fields per column box, type a number greater than zero, and the page fields are rearranged into columns, with the specified number of page fields in each column. With this page layout option, page fields fill down for the number of fields specified in the Fields per column option, then start filling the next column of fields.

Note If the Fields per column option is set at zero, the page fields are arranged in a single column.

For example, with five page fields, if you opt to have two fields per column, page fields one and two will be in the first column of page fields, three and four will be in the next column, and five will be in the third column.

Over, then Down

When Over, then Down is selected, the option that follows is Fields per row. In the Fields per row box, type a number greater than zero, and the page fields are rearranged into rows, with the specified number of page fields in each row. With this page layout option, page fields fill across for the number of fields specified in the Fields per row option, then start filling the next row of fields.

■**Note** If the Fields per row option is set at zero, the page fields are arranged in a single row.

For example, with five page fields, if you opt to have two fields per row, page fields one and two will be in the first row of page fields, three and four will be in the next row, and five will be in the third row.

1.37. Understanding PivotTable Options: Fields per Column/Fields per Row

Problem

Your PivotTable has several page fields, and they use a great deal of space at the top of the worksheet, which makes it harder to work with your pivot table. You'd like to arrange the page fields horizontally instead of vertically so that they use fewer rows.

Solution

The name of this option depends on the selection made in the Page layout option above it. Type or select a number, between 0 and 255, in the Fields per column/Fields per row box to control the page field layout. If the Fields per column option is set at zero, the page fields are arranged in a single column. If the Fields per row option is set at zero, the page fields are arranged in a single row.

1.38. Understanding PivotTable Options: Error Values

Problem

Your pivot table is showing error values, and you'd rather have the cells show as blank.

Solution

By default, error values are displayed in a pivot table. For example, if you create a calculated item, the pivot table may show a #DIV/0! error if it has to divide by zero. You can use the For error values, show option to display something other than the error value.

■**Note** This setting only affects cells in the data area of the pivot table. If error values in the source data appear in the row, column, or page area, they will not be replaced.

To turn the option on, add a checkmark in the check box. Then, in the text box, type the value you want in the error cells. You can use text, or characters such as dashes, to replace the errors. For example, you could replace errors with two hyphen characters (--) or with the text N/A.

■**Note** If you use a single hyphen in the text box, the error values will be replaced with zeros.

Up to 255 characters are allowed, but a short message is best in most cases.

■**Tip** If you'd like the error cells to appear blank, leave the For error values, show text box empty.

1.39. Understanding PivotTable Options: Empty Cells

Problem

Your pivot table has empty cells in the data area, and you'd like to use dashes instead.

Solution

By default, empty cells in the data area are left blank. If your pivot table's row area has a Regions field, and your pivot table's column area has a Products field, there may be blank cells in the data area if some products were not sold in some regions. You can use the For empty cells, show option to display something other than the blank cells.

Note This setting only affects cells in the data area of the pivot table. If empty cells in the source data appear in the row, column, or page area as (blank), they will not be replaced.

To turn the option on, add a checkmark in the check box. Then, in the text box, type the value you want in the empty cells. You can use text, or characters such as dashes, to replace the errors. For example, you could replace empty cells with two hyphen characters (--) or with the text N/A. Up to 255 characters are allowed, but a short message is best in most cases.

Note If you turn off the For empty cells, show option, or use a single hyphen in the text box, the empty cells will be filled with zeros.

1.40. Understanding PivotTable Options: Set Print Titles

Problem

You want to print the pivot table with the row and heading columns on every page.

Solution

Turn on the Set print titles option, and the page, row, and column headings will appear on every sheet when you print the pivot table. You can rearrange the pivot table in any layout without manually resetting the print titles, and the headings will always appear on the printed sheets.

Note For best results when using the Set print titles option, the worksheet shouldn't contain other data.

1. Before you turn on this option, choose File ➤ Page Setup.

2. On the Sheet tab, clear the Rows to repeat at top and Columns to repeat at left boxes.

■**Caution** If there is an entry in either of these boxes, the Set print titles option won't be applied. If you clear the Print titles settings, on the Sheet tab in the Page Setup dialog box, after turning on the Set print titles option, you'll have to turn the Set print titles option off, then turn it back on, for it to take effect.

3. Click OK to close the Page Setup dialog box.

4. Right-click on a cell in the PivotTable, choose Table Options, and add a checkmark to Set print titles.

■**Tip** If you clear the Print titles settings after turning on the Set print titles option, you'll have to turn the Set print titles option off, then turn it back on, for it to take effect.

1.41. Understanding PivotTable Options: Mark Totals with *

Problem

The Mark totals with * option isn't available for my pivot table.

Solution

If your pivot table is based on a non-OLAP data source, the Mark Totals with * option isn't available.

If your pivot table is based on an OLAP source, each total has an asterisk to indicate that the amount includes both visible and hidden items. To remove the asterisks, clear the check box for this option. If the option is disabled for a pivot table based on an OLAP source, click the Include Hidden Items in Totals button on the PivotTable toolbar.

1.42. Understanding PivotTable Options: Save Data with Table Layout

Problem

What are the benefits of using the Save data with table layout option?

Solution

When using an external source, you can specify whether or not to save the data with the table layout. If you turn this option off, the file will be smaller, and may open, close, and save faster. However, you'll have to refresh the pivot table before you can use it.

If you turn this option on, the file size will be larger, and it may open, close and save more slowly. However, you don't have to refresh the pivot table in order to use it. If storage space isn't a concern, I'd recommend turning this option on.

For example, a sample file saved with data was 1125KB, and the same file saved without data was 343KB. The difference in file opening and closing times was indiscernible, but the pivot table with the Save data with table layout option turned off had to be refreshed before it was used.

1.43. Understanding PivotTable Options: Enable Drill to Details

Problem

What are the benefits of using the Enable drill to details option?

Solution

This option allows users to double-click on a pivot table cell, and show or hide detail. If you double-click a data cell, a new sheet is inserted in the workbook, containing the data from the source table, in the same field layout as the source. The formatting for AutoFormat List 3 is applied to the detail data.

■Note This option isn't available for OLAP-based pivot tables.

How It Works

When the Enable drill to details option is turned on, if you double-click a row or column cell, details for inner fields are shown or hidden. If the field has no inner fields, a dialog box appears, asking you to select from a list of the pivot table's fields. The selected field is added to the pivot table as an inner field of the double-clicked field, and the details for the double-clicked cell are shown.

If you double-click a row or column heading cell for which the inner field items are visible, the inner field items are hidden.

If you turn off the Enable drill to details option, and users double-click on a cell in the pivot table's data area, they'll see an error message that warns them the pivot table cannot be changed (see Figure 1-4).

Figure 1-4. *The error message warning users the pivot table cannot be changed*

1.44. Understanding PivotTable Options: Refresh on Open

Problem

What are the benefits of using the Refresh on open option?

Solution

Turn this option on if you want the pivot table to be automatically refreshed when the workbook is opened. This should ensure that users don't mistakenly view outdated data, but may slow the opening of the workbook.

For pivot tables based on an external source, if this option is on, when you open the workbook you may see an alert message advising that queries may be harmful (see Figure 1-5). Whether you see the message depends on your Excel security level.

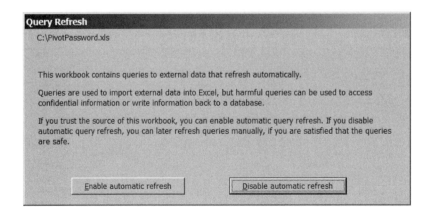

Figure 1-5. *The Refresh on Open message*

If others will be using your pivot table workbook, you can warn them that this message will appear, and explain why, so they'll be comfortable enabling the query refresh. Otherwise, they may see stale data, and could make incorrect decisions based on that data.

1.45. Understanding PivotTable Options: Refresh Every *n* Minutes

Problem

What are the benefits of using the Refresh every *n* minutes option?

Solution

Turn this option on if you want the pivot table to be automatically refreshed at a specific interval while the workbook is open. You can use this option if the source data changes frequently, and it's important that the pivot table reflect the latest available data.

■Note This option is only available for pivot tables with an external data source.

1.46. Understanding PivotTable Options: Save Password

Problem

What are the benefits of using the Save password option?

Solution

If the pivot table's external data source requires a password, you can turn on this option to store the password with the pivot table. However, security concerns may deter you from using this option.

If you turn this option off, you'll be prompted for the password during the first refresh in a session with the pivot table workbook (see Figure 1-6).

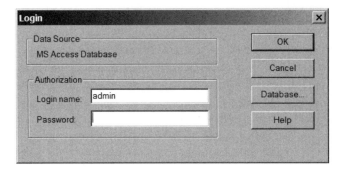

Figure 1-6. *Password prompt for an external data source*

1.47. Understanding PivotTable Options: Background Query

Problem

What are the benefits of using the Background query option?

Solution

If you turn this option on, you can continue to work while Excel runs the query for the external data source. However, if you are refreshing the pivot table as part of running a series of macros, you may need to wait until the pivot table is refreshed before continuing with the remainder of the code. In that case, leave the option off to ensure that the pivot table is refreshed before other operations occur.

■**Note** This option isn't available for OLAP-based pivot tables.

1.48. Understanding PivotTable Options: Optimize Memory

Problem

Your pivot table is based on an external data source, and you wonder if you should use the Optimize memory option.

Solution

■**Note** This option isn't available for OLAP-based pivot tables.

You can leave this option turned off, unless you receive an error that warns of insufficient memory when working with the PivotTable report. When the option is turned on, refreshing the pivot table is much slower. For example, with a pivot table based on an Access query with 30,000 records, the pivot table refreshed in under 3 seconds with the Optimize memory option turned off. When the option was turned on, the refresh took over 10 seconds.

How It Works

This option was introduced in Excel 97 to address memory problems that occurred when creating pivot tables in earlier versions of Excel. When the option is on, Excel queries the external data if the pivot table is refreshed, or the layout is changed, to determine how many unique items are in each field. If there are 256 or fewer items, it can optimize the storage for that field. However, running the queries has a negative impact on the pivot table performance, and the Optimize memory option should only be turned on if memory errors occur.

1.49. Understanding Pivot Table Layout

Problem

In Step 3 of the PivotTable and PivotChart Wizard, should you click the Layout button, and create the layout there, or should you use the worksheet to create the pivot table layout?

Solution

Create the layout on the worksheet if field names are long, or there are several fields—it's easier to see the fields in the field list than in the wizard.

Use the Layout dialog box in the PivotTable and PivotChart Wizard if field names are short and there aren't too many fields; it may be quicker because the pivot table isn't created until you leave the PivotTable and PivotChart Wizard.

▓**Tip** Place fields with more items in the row area, where they can fill down, rather than in the column area, where they will fill across. Even if the number of items doesn't exceed the number of columns on the worksheet, it's usually easier to absorb information in a narrower layout.

CHAPTER 2

■ ■ ■

Sorting and Grouping Pivot Table Data

As you analyze data in a pivot table, you may want to rearrange the items in the Row and Column fields, or sort the summarized data, to focus on products that are selling the best, or regions that are doing poorly. Sort the fields or the data to move the important information to the top.

2.1. Sorting a Pivot Field: One Row Field

Problem

Your pivot table contains the field Product in the row area, and the field Sum of Sold in the data area, as Figure 2-1 shows. You want to sort the data in descending order, so the products with the highest revenue appear at the top of the pivot table.

	A	B
1	Category	(All) ▼
2		
3	Sum of Sold	
4	Product ▼	Total
5	Arrowroot	510,006.40
6	Banana	1,301,146.59
7	Bran	1,139,388.03
8	Carrot	1,251,670.50

Figure 2-1. *The Product row field and Sum of Sold data field*

Solution

You can quickly sort the data by using a toolbar button, or you can change the Product field settings.

Quickly Sorting by the Sum of Sold Data

1. Select a cell in the data area in the Sum of Sold column.

2. On the Standard toolbar, click the Sort Descending button (Z-A).

■**Note** This technique sets the Product field to Manual sort. If you refresh the pivot table, the Sum of Sold column will not automatically re-sort, so the data may no longer be in descending order. You might have to click the Sort Descending button again to see data in the correct order.

Setting the Sort Order for the Product Field

1. Right-click on the Product field button, and choose Field Settings.

2. Click the Advanced button to open the PivotTable Field Advanced Options dialog box.

3. Under AutoSort options, select Descending.

4. From the Using field dropdown list, select the Sum of Sold field (see Figure 2-2).

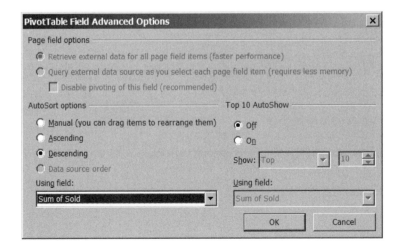

Figure 2-2. *The Using field dropdown list*

5. Click OK to close the PivotTable Field Advanced Options dialog box, and click OK to close the PivotTable Field dialog box.

Note With this AutoSort option selected, the Product field will automatically re-sort in descending order when the pivot table is refreshed.

2.2. Sorting a Pivot Field: Outer Row Field

Problem

There are two fields in the row area of your pivot table: Salesperson and Category, as shown in Figure 2-3. Salesperson, the outer row field, is sorted alphabetically, and you want to sort the salespeople in descending order by their total sales.

Note If a pivot table has more than one field in the row area, the field that's closest to the data area is the inner field. All the remaining row fields are outer fields. In Figure 2-3, Salesperson is the outer row field, and Category is the inner row field.

	A	B	C
1	Customer	(All) ▼	
2			
3	Sum of Sold		
4	Salesperson ▼	Category ▼	Total
5	Boston	Bars	330,646.80
6		Cookies	252,625.99
7		Crackers	595,109.97
8	Boston Total		1,178,382.76
9	Lee	Bars	225,745.17
10		Cookies	167,482.21
11		Crackers	392,037.47
12	Lee Total		785,264.85
13	Parent	Bars	328,327.02
14		Cookies	255,501.08
15		Crackers	578,699.22
16	Parent Total		1,162,527.32
17	Grand Total		3,126,174.93

Figure 2-3. *Salesperson is the outer row field and Category is the inner row field.*

Solution

To sort the outer field in descending order by subtotal, follow these steps:

1. Double-click the field button for the outer field in the row area—the Salesperson field in this example.

2. In the PivotTable Field dialog box that opens, click the Advanced button.

3. In the PivotTable Field Advanced Options dialog box, under the AutoSort options, select Descending.

4. From the Using field dropdown list, select the field on which you want to base the sort—Sum of Sold in this example.

5. Click OK to close the PivotTable Field Advanced Options dialog box, and click OK to close the PivotTable Field dialog box.

This will sort the Salesperson subtotals in descending order.

Tip The subtotals do not have to be visible in order to sort by them.

How It Works

When you do a descending sort, values are sorted in the following order:

1. Error values such as #N/A and #NAME?

2. Logical values (TRUE comes before FALSE)

3. Text, in the following order: Z Y X W V U T S R Q P O N M L K J I H G F E D C B A > = < + ~ } | { ` _ ^] \ [@ ? ; : / . , *) (& % $ # " ! (space) 9 8 7 6 5 4 3 2 1 0

Tip Hyphens and apostrophes are ignored, except where two items are the same except for a hyphen. In that case, in a descending sort the item with the hyphen is sorted first.

---

4. Numbers (including dates, which Excel stores as numbers)

5. Blank cells

■**Note** Unlike a worksheet sort, where error values are treated equally, error values in a pivot table are sorted alphabetically.

2.3. Sorting a Pivot Field: Inner Row Field

Problem

There are two fields, Salesperson and Customer, in the row area of your pivot table. You want to sort the inner row field, Customer, in descending order, to highlight the best customers for each salesperson, based on Sales Dollars.

Solution

When you sort the inner row field (Customer), the results will be sorted within the related outer field (Salesperson). The order of the outer fields won't be affected by sorting the inner field.

1. Double-click the field button for the inner field—the Product field in this example.

2. In the PivotTable Field dialog box that opens, click the Advanced button.

3. In the PivotTable Field Advanced Options dialog box, under the AutoSort options, select Descending.

4. From the Using field dropdown list, select the field on which you want to base the sort—Sum of Sales Dollars in this example.

5. Click OK to close the PivotTable Field Advanced Options dialog box, and click OK to close the PivotTable Field dialog box.

The order of the items in the Salesperson field doesn't change, but the Customers for each Salesperson are sorted in descending order.

How It Works

In a pivot table, when you do an ascending sort, values are sorted in the following order:

1. Numbers (including dates, which Excel stores as numbers)

2. Text, in the following order: 0 1 2 3 4 5 6 7 8 9 (space) ! " # $ % & ( ) * , . / : ; ? @ [\ ] ^ _ ` { | } ~ + < = > A B C D E F G H I J K L M N O P Q R S T U V W X Y Z

Tip Hyphens and apostrophes are ignored, except where two items are the same except for a hyphen. In that case, in an ascending sort the item with the hyphen is sorted last.

3. Logical values (FALSE comes before TRUE)

4. Error values such as #N/A and #NAME?

5. Blank cells

2.4. Sorting a Pivot Field: Renamed Numeric Items

Problem

You accidentally renamed an item, changing it from 3.00 to 3.01, and now it's not sorting correctly. When you refresh the pivot table, the item doesn't change back to its original value.

Solution

If you rename a numeric item in the pivot table, it becomes text, and is sorted after the numbers (or before the numbers in a descending sort). To change the entry back to a number, follow these steps:

1. Drag the numeric field out of the pivot table.

2. Refresh the pivot table.

3. Drag the numeric field back to the pivot table.

2.5. Sorting a Pivot Field: New Items Out of Order

Problem

You added several new products to your pivot table source data, and when you refreshed the pivot table, the new products appear at the end of the dropdown list.

Solution

If the Product field is set to Manual sort, new items will appear at the end of the drop-down list. If you sort the field, the dropdown list will also be sorted. Follow these steps to sort the field:

1. Select a cell in the Product field.

2. Click the Sort Ascending (A-Z) button on the Excel Standard toolbar.

If you want new products to automatically appear in alphabetical order, you can set the Products field to AutoSort:

1. Double-click the Product field button.

2. In the PivotTable Field dialog box that opens, click the Advanced button.

3. In the PivotTable Field Advanced Options dialog box, under the AutoSort options, select Ascending.

4. From the Using field dropdown list, select Product.

5. Click OK to close the PivotTable Field Advanced Options dialog box, and click OK to close the PivotTable Field dialog box.

2.6. Sorting a Pivot Field: Sorting Items Geographically

Problem

You have a Regions field in the row area, and you would like the items sorted geographically (east to west) instead of alphabetically.

Solution

In Excel, you can create custom lists, similar to the built-in lists of weekdays and months. The custom list can be based on a worksheet list, or typed in the Options dialog box.

Creating a Custom List

1. Choose Tools ➤ Options.

2. On the Custom Lists tab, select the NEW LIST item.

3. Click in the List entries box and type your list, pressing the Enter key to separate the items (see Figure 2-4).

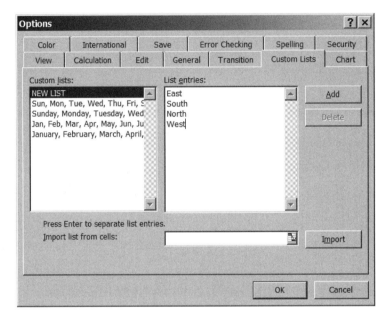

Figure 2-4. *Create a custom list by typing the entries.*

▦**Tip** Instead of typing a list in the List entries box, you can import the list from the worksheet by selecting it and clicking the Import button.

---

4. Click OK to close the Options dialog box.

Applying the Custom Sort Order

If the Region field is already in the pivot table, it won't automatically be sorted in the new custom order. If the field is set for AutoSort, with Region selected in the Using field drop-down list, refresh the pivot table to see the Regions in the custom sort order.

If the Region field is set for manual sort, you can remove it from the pivot table, refresh the pivot table, then drag the Region field back. Or use the custom sort order to re-sort it:

1. Select the Region field button.

2. Choose Data ➤ Sort. If the field is set for AutoSort, you'll see a message asking if you want to sort it manually. Click the No button, then refresh the pivot table to apply the custom sort order (see Figure 2-5).

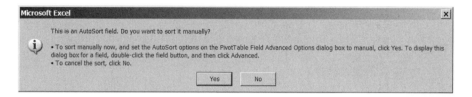

Figure 2-5. *Warning message that appears if the field is set for AutoSort*

3. The Sort dialog box appears, with fewer options than you'd have when choosing Data ➤ Sort in a list on the worksheet (see Figure 2.6). Under the Sort option, Labels should be selected, because you had selected a label cell in the pivot table.

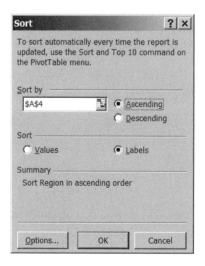

Figure 2-6. *The Sort dialog box when accessed from a pivot table*

4. Click the Options button to open the Sort Options dialog box.

5. From the First key sort order dropdown list, select your custom list, then click OK.

6. Click OK to close the Sort dialog box.

2.7. Sorting a Pivot Field: Data Source Order

Problem

When you created a new PivotTable report, the field items were listed in ascending order. You want the items in the same order they appear in the source data, but when you right-click a field and click the Advanced button, the Data Source Order option is disabled, and you can't select it.

Solution

In the PivotTable Field Advanced Options dialog box, the Data Source Order option is available only for pivot tables based on OLAP source data. For pivot tables built from non-OLAP sources, the items are listed in ascending order when the pivot table is created. To achieve a different sort order, you could create a custom list, as described in Section 2.6, and sort on that.

2.8. Sorting a Pivot Field When Some Items Won't Sort Correctly

Problem

One of your salespeople is named Jan, and her name always appears at the top of the SalesRep items, ahead of the names that precede it alphabetically.

Solution

If the field is set to Manual sort, Jan should move to the correct position alphabetically. Follow these steps to set the field for Manual sort:

1. Right-click the SalesRep field button, and choose Field Settings.

2. Click the Advanced button.

3. Under AutoSort options, select Manual.

4. Click OK to close the PivotTable Field Advanced Options dialog box, and click OK to close the PivotTable Field dialog box.

5. Select a cell in the SalesRep field, and click the Sort Ascending (A-Z) button on the Excel Standard toolbar.

How It Works

Jan goes to the top of the list because Excel assumes it means January, which appears in one of the built-in custom lists. Other names, such as May or June, would also go to the top of the list, because they're also in the custom list for months.

When you create a pivot table and Excel detects an entry from a custom list, it uses that list as the first sort order. So, in your table, Jan sorts to the top, and the other SalesRep names appear below, because they're not in a custom list.

2.9. Using Top 10 AutoShow: Specifying Top Items Overall

Problem

In the row area, you have Region and Product fields, and you'd like to show the top ten products overall.

Solution

For non-OLAP based pivot tables, if you have multiple fields in the row area, the top ten products per region will be displayed. For OLAP-based pivot tables, the results for the top ten products overall will be displayed, with the sales per region showing.

In the non-OLAP pivot table, you could remove the Region field from the row area, and the top ten overall products would show. If you move Region to the column area, the pivot table would show the top ten overall products, with the sales results for each region in its column.

2.10. Using Top 10 AutoShow: Specifying Items Over a Set Amount

Problem

You'd like to use the Top 10 AutoShow feature to show the products that have sales over a set amount.

Solution

The Top 10 AutoShow feature can show only a set number of items, not items that meet a specific criterion. You can manually or programmatically hide the items that are below your limit.

2.11. Using Top 10 AutoShow: Referring to a Cell Value

Problem

You'd like to use a cell value to set the number of items in the Top 10 AutoShow feature.

Solution

You could use programming to change the AutoShow settings, based on a change to the worksheet. However, you can't manually refer to a cell while in the Top 10 AutoShow dialog box.

2.12. Grouping: Error Message When Grouping Items in a Date Field

Problem

You get an error message when you try to group the items in your date field (see Figure 2-7).

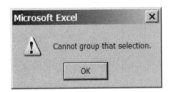

Figure 2-7. *The error message you see when items in a field can't be grouped*

Solution

This error occurs if there are blank cells, or cells with text, in the source data field.

1. If there are blank cells in the date column of the source data, add a date in each record. If necessary, add dummy dates where no date is available.

2. If any of the rows contain text, such as N/A, replace the text with a date.

3. Check the source range in the PivotTable and PivotChart Wizard to ensure that no blank rows have been included at the end of the source data table.

4. Refresh the pivot table, and try to group the items in the date field.

Tip If you're still unable to group the items in the date field, remove it from the pivot table layout, refresh the pivot table, then add the date field to the pivot table again.

2.13. Grouping: Error Message When Grouping Items in a Numeric Field

Problem

You get an error message when you try to group the items in your numeric field.

Solution

The numbers may have been copied or imported from another program and are text values instead of real numbers. In the source data, convert the text to numbers, and you'll be able to group the items in the pivot table.

How It Works

There are several ways to convert text "numbers" to real numbers. For example, you can use the Paste Special command:

1. Select a blank cell on the worksheet, and copy it.

2. In the source data, select the cells that contain the numbers.

3. Choose Edit ➤ Paste Special.

4. Select Add, and click OK.

Another method is to use the Text to Columns feature:

1. Select the cells that contain the numbers.

2. Choose Data ➤ Text to Columns.

3. Click the Finish button.

2.14. Grouping: Error Message When Grouping Items in a Date Field with No Blanks or Text

Problem

You've checked your source data, and it doesn't contain any blank cells or text values in the date column. However, you still get an error message when you try to group the items in your date field.

Solution

There may be a field with grouped items left over from the previous time that you grouped the data. Check the field list to see if there's a second copy of the date field, for example, Date2.

If there is, add it to the row area and ungroup the items. Then, you should be able to group the date field items again.

2.15. Grouping the Items in a Page Field

Problem

Your date field is in the page area, and you aren't able to group the items in the field.

Solution

Move the date field to the row or column area and group the items, then drag the date field back to the page area.

2.16. Grouping the Items in a Page Field: Using an External Source

Problem

Your date field is in the page area, and you aren't able to move it to the row area.

Solution

If you're using an external source, check that the page field can be moved:

1. Double-click the Page field button.

2. In the PivotTable Field dialog box, click the Advanced button.

3. Set the Page field option to Retrieve external data for all page field items.

4. Click OK to close the PivotTable Field Advanced Options dialog box, and click OK to close the PivotTable Field dialog box.

2.17. Grouping: Incorrect Error Message About Calculated Items

Problem

You're trying to group the items in a date field, and you're getting an error message about calculated items. The date field doesn't have any calculated items.

Solution

There may be another field in the pivot table that has a calculated item, and that's preventing the grouping. The other field may not be visible in the pivot table, but it will still prevent the grouping. You can delete the calculated item, or use formulas in the source data to create date groups. Then, add that field to the pivot table.

2.18. Grouping Text Items

Problem

You'd like to group states by region, but you don't want to do it manually.

Solution

Instead of grouping the items in the pivot table, you could add a Region field to the source data. Then, add that field as the first row field, and the states will appear in the correct region.

2.19. Grouping Dates by Week

Problem

You want to group dates by week, but the option isn't available in the Group By dialog box.

Solution

In the Group By dialog box, select Days, and set the number of days to seven.

2.20. Grouping Dates by Fiscal Quarter

Problem

You want to group dates by fiscal quarter instead of using the calendar quarter that's available in the Group By dialog box.

Solution

There's no built-in option to group by fiscal quarter. In the source data, you can add a column that calculates the fiscal quarter, then add that field to the pivot table.

2.21. Grouping Renamed Numeric Items

Problem

You renamed an item, changing it from 3.00 to 3.01, and now you get an unusual error message when you try to group the items (see Figure 2-8).

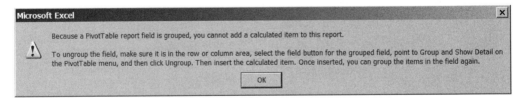

Figure 2-8. *The error message that appears when you try to group items in the field with the renamed item*

Solution

If you rename a numeric item in the pivot table, it becomes text, and will prevent you from grouping items in the numeric field. Follow these steps to change the entry back to a number:

1. Drag the numeric field out of the pivot table.

2. Refresh the pivot table.

3. Drag the numeric field back to the pivot table.

2.22. Grouping Months

Problem

When you group by month, January data from different years is lumped together. You'd like to keep the data from different years separated.

Solution

When you group, select both Year and Month in the Group By list. The data from each year will be grouped, and each month in that year will be grouped.

2.23. Grouping Dates Using the Starting Date

Problem

You want to group dates into four-week periods that coincide with your sales calendar. The grouped dates are a couple of days off, starting midweek instead of on a Monday.

Solution

When you group the dates, select to group by days, and set the number of days to 28. Then, select a starting date for the first period.

How It Works

Excel automatically selects the first date in your source data, but you can select a date outside this range to get the starting date that you need.

2.24. Grouping Dates by Months and Weeks

Problem

You grouped days by week, and the date range was displayed in the pivot table. When you added month as a grouping level, the days became ungrouped, but you'd like to use months and weeks together.

Solution

There's no way to group by both weeks and months. You could create a column in the source data, and calculate one of the grouping levels there. Then, add that field to the pivot table.

2.25. Grouping the Items in a Pivot Table Based on an Existing Pivot Table

Problem

You based one pivot table on another. You'd like to group items in one pivot table, and leave items in that field ungrouped in the other pivot table.

Solution

Because the pivot tables use the same pivot cache, the grouped items will be the same in both tables. If you need different groups in the pivot tables, you can base each pivot table on the source range instead of using another pivot table as the source.

2.26. Grouping Dates Outside the Range

Problem

When you group by date, and set a start or end date, Excel automatically creates categories for all items outside this range. You'd like to prevent this from happening.

Solution

There's no setting you can change to prevent this from happening. You can uncheck these groups in the date field dropdown list to prevent them from appearing in the pivot table.

2.27. Grouping Nonadjacent Items

Problem

You want to group several customers in the Customer row field, but they aren't listed consecutively. You don't want to rearrange the pivot items before you group them.

Solution

1. In the Customer field, select one of the cells that contains a customer name that you want in the group.

2. Ctrl-click on each of the remaining customer names for the group (see Figure 2-9).

3		
4	Sum of Sold	
5	Customer ▼	Total
6	Corner Cabin	1,704,322.23
7	Dependable Druggist	1,595,535.06
8	Discount Daze	1,583,869.63
9	Food Franchise	1,605,831.36
10	Friendly Pharmacy	1,582,668.72
11	Giant Grocer	1,583,829.88
12	Magna Mart ✛	1,590,328.22
13	Value Variety	1,551,432.46
14	Grand Total	12,797,817.56

Figure 2-9. *Hold the Ctrl key and click on customer names.*

3. Right-click on one of the selected Customer names, and choose Group and Show Detail ➤ Group.

Calculations in a Pivot Table

In a pivot table, you can use summary functions or custom calculations to summarize the data, and you can write your own formulas to create calculated fields and calculated items.

3.1. Using Summary Functions

Problem

You can select from a list of summary functions when subtotaling fields in a pivot table or adding fields to the data area, and you wonder if they're the same as the worksheet functions.

Solution

When you add a field to the pivot table, a list of 11 functions is available to summarize the data in the data area or subtotal the data for row and column fields. The summary functions in a pivot table are similar to the worksheet functions with the same names, with a few differences as noted in the "How It Works" section that follows.

A summary function is automatically applied to each field when it's added to the pivot table, and in most cases you can select a different summary function.

Note The list of summary functions is not available when you're working with OLAP-based pivot tables.

Follow these steps to change the summary function for a field in the data area:

1. Right-click a cell in the field that you want to change, and choose Field Settings.

2. In the Summarize by list, select one of the functions (see Figure 3-1).

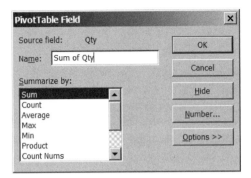

Figure 3-1. *The PivotTable Field dialog box with a list of summary functions*

3. Click OK to close the PivotTable Field dialog box.

▧**Tip** Add two copies of a field to the pivot table data area, and use a different summary function for each copy. For example, show the Sum of Orders and the Count of Orders.

How It Works

Only the 11 functions listed here are available when summarizing or subtotaling pivot table data; other functions, such as Median, Mode, and Percentile, can be calculated from the source data, outside the pivot table.

Sum

Sum is the default summary function for numerical fields that are added to the pivot table's data area, and it totals all the underlying values in the data area. The result is the same as using the SUM function on the worksheet to total the values.

Count

Count is the default summary function when fields with text or blank cells are added to the data area. Like the COUNTA worksheet function, the pivot table Count function counts text, numbers, and errors. Blank cells are not counted.

Average

This summary function totals all the underlying values in the data area, and divides by the number of values. The result is the same as using the AVERAGE function on the worksheet to calculate the average (mean) of the values.

Max

This summary function shows the maximum value from the underlying values in the data area. The result is the same as using the MAX function on the worksheet to calculate the maximum of the values.

Min

This summary function shows the minimum value from the underlying values in the data area. The result is the same as using the MIN function on the worksheet to calculate the minimum of the values.

Product

This summary function shows the result of multiplying all the underlying values in the data area. The result is the same as using the PRODUCT function on the worksheet to calculate the product of the values. The results of this function may be very large numbers and default to a Scientific number format. Excel only stores and calculates with 15 significant digits of precision, so after the 15th character you'll only see zeros.

Count Nums

This summary function counts all the underlying numbers in the data area. The result is the same as using the COUNT function on the worksheet. Blank cells, errors, and text are not counted.

StDev

Like the STDEV worksheet function, this summary function calculates the standard deviation for the underlying data in the data area.

If the count of items is one, a #DIV/0! error will be displayed, because one is subtracted from the count when calculating the standard deviation.

In Excel 2003, there may be differences between the worksheet results and the pivot table results, because the worksheet function has been improved. For more information, see the Microsoft Knowledge Base article "Description of Improvements in the Statistical

Functions in Excel 2003 and in Excel 2004 for Mac," at http://support.microsoft.com/default.aspx?kbid=828888.

StDevp

Like the STDEVP worksheet function, the StDevp summary function calculates the standard deviation for the entire population for the underlying data in the data area. In Excel 2003, improvements were made to several statistical functions, including STDEV and STDEVP. See the previous "StDev" section for more information.

Var

Like the VAR worksheet function, this summary function calculates the variance for the underlying data in the data area.

  If the count of items is one, a #DIV/0! error will be displayed, because one is subtracted from the count when calculating the standard deviation.

  In Excel 2003, improvements were made to several statistical functions, including VAR and VARP. The Var and Varp summary functions have been improved when used in the interior of the PivotTable report, but not for grand totals for rows or columns. For more information, see the Microsoft Knowledge Base article "Excel Statistical Functions: VAR and VARP Improvements and Pivot Tables," at http://support.microsoft.com/default.aspx?kbid=829250.

Varp

This summary function calculates the variance for the entire population for the underlying data in the data area. In Excel 2003, improvements were made to several statistical functions, including VAR and VARP. See the previous "Var" section for more information.

Errors in the Source Data

The Count and Count Nums fields handle errors as we outlined earlier. For other summary functions, if there are errors in the source data field, the first error encountered will be displayed in the pivot table, and the total will not be calculated. If subtotals, or row and column totals, are displayed, affected totals and subtotals will display the error.

  For example, the source data shown in Figure 3-2 has two errors for West Binder data—a #REF! error and an #N/A error.

C	D	E	F	G
Region	Item	Cost	Units	Total
East	Pencil	2.99	95	284.05
West	Binder	#REF!	50	#REF!
West	Pencil	2.99	36	107.64
West	Binder	#N/A	27	#N/A
West	Pencil	2.99	56	167.44

Figure 3-2. *Errors in the sample source data*

The first error, #REF!, appears in the pivot table, when West Binder Totals are summed (see Figure 3-3). If the dates were sorted in descending order, the #N/A error would be listed first, and would appear in the PivotTable report.

Sum of Total	Region ▼			
Item ▼	West	Central	East	Grand Total
Binder	#REF!	973	1,831	#REF!
Desk	825	1,925		2,750
Pencil	595	1,094	451	2,141
Pen Set		729	1,243	1,971
Pen	151		348	499
Grand Total	#REF!	4,721	3,874	#REF!

Figure 3-3. *The first error in the source data appears in the pivot table.*

3.2. Using Summary Functions: Default Functions

Problem

When you added the Amount_Owing field to the data area, it automatically used the Sum function, but when you added the Amount_Paid field to the data area, it automatically used the Count function. You're not sure why different functions were used for two data fields that are similar.

Solution

Perhaps there were blank cells in the source data for the Amount_Paid field. If you add a number field to the data area, the default summary function is Sum. If there are blank cells, or non-numeric data in the field, the Count function is used as a default.

Note You can't set a default summary function in a PivotTable.

After the field has been added to the data area, you can change its summary function:

1. Right-click a cell in the field that you want to change, and choose Field Settings.

2. In the Summarize by list, select one of the functions.

3. Click OK to close the PivotTable Field dialog box.

3.3. Using Summary Functions: Counting Blank Cells

Problem

There are blank cells in the Region field of your source data, and you want to show a count of the blank Region cells in the pivot table. You added the Region field to the pivot table's row area, and another copy of the Region field in the data area, as Count of Region. However, there's no count showing for the blank regions.

Solution

A pivot table can't count the blank cells when you add a field to the data area and use the Count or CountNum summary function. Add a different field to the data area, and use it for the count. For example, if the Units field will always contain data, add Region to the row area, and add Count of Units to the data area (see Figure 3-4). The count of blank Regions will be calculated.

Region ▼	Data ▼	
	Count of Units	Count of Region
Central	14	14
East	8	8
West	18	18
(blank)	3	
Grand Total	43	40

Figure 3-4. *Blank cells are not counted in the data area.*

3.4. Using Custom Calculations: Difference From

Problem

Every morning, you download the current month's sales data from your sales system. You'd like to use the pivot table to calculate each day's change from the previous day, to obtain the daily sales figures for each region.

In your pivot table, Date is in the row area, and Region is in the column area. Units sold (Sum of Units) is in the data area, as shown in Figure 3-5.

Sum of Units	Region ▼			
Date ▼	Central	East	West	Grand Total
8/10/2006	1349	1666	2043	5058
8/11/2006	1563	1899	2562	6024
8/14/2006	1957	2697	2967	7621
Grand Total	4869	6262	7572	18703

Figure 3-5. *Pivot table shows units sold to date for each region*

Solution

To supplement the summary functions, custom calculations are available when summarizing data in a pivot table. In addition to the default normal calculation, custom calculations provide eight different ways of viewing the summary results. For this problem, use the Difference From custom calculation to analyze the data that accumulates over the month by comparing each day's total to the previous day's total.

■Tip Custom calculations are only available for pivot tables based on non-OLAP sources.

---

1. Right-click on the Sum of Units button, and choose Field Settings.

2. Click the Options button.

3. From the dropdown list for Show data as, select Difference From.

4. For the base field, select Date.

■Caution If you select a base field that isn't in the row or column area, all the results will show an #N/A error.

---

5. For the Base item, select (previous), and click the OK button.

The row for the first date is empty, because there's no previous date with which to compare it. The remaining rows show the change from the previous day in units sold for each region (see Figure 3-6).

Sum of Units	Region ▼			
Date ▼	Central	East	West	Grand Total
8/10/2006				
8/11/2006	214	233	519	966
8/14/2006	394	798	405	1597
Grand Total				

Figure 3-6. *The custom calculation Difference From compares daily sales totals.*

How It Works

The Difference From custom calculation compares each item in the field to another item in the same field. In this example, (previous) was selected, so each day's total is compared to the previous day's total. If days are missing or hidden, the comparison is made to the previous visible day.

Instead of (previous), you could select (next) to compare each day to the next visible day's totals, or select a specific date to compare all days to the sales for the selected date.

Using the same sample data, you could select Region as the base field, and compare each region's sales to sales in the Central Region (see Figure 3-7).

Sum of Units	Region ▼			
Date ▼	Central	East	West	Grand Total
8/10/2006		317	694	
8/11/2006		336	999	
8/14/2006		740	1010	
Grand Total		1393	2703	

Figure 3-7. *The custom calculation Difference From, with Region as a base field*

3.5. Using Custom Calculations: % Of

Problem

You have monthly sales figures for each region, and would like to compare average sales for each region to the average sales in your strongest region.

In your pivot table, Date is in the row area, grouped by Month; Region is in the column area; and Units sold (Average of Units) is in the data area (see Figure 3-8).

Average of Units	Region ▼			
Date ▼	Central	East	West	Grand Total
Jan	606	439	606	561
Feb	455	746	439	571
Mar	542	651	503	578
Apr	429	351	283	355
Grand Total	517	553	454	510

Figure 3-8. *Pivot table with average Units per Sale per Region*

Solution

While using the custom calculations, you can use different summary functions for the data. For this problem, you can use the Average summary function and the % Of custom calculation.

1. Right-click on the Sum of Units button, and choose Field Settings.

2. Click the Options button.

3. From the dropdown list for Show data as, select % Of.

4. For the Base field, select Region.

5. For the Base item, select Central (see Figure 3-9), then click the OK button.

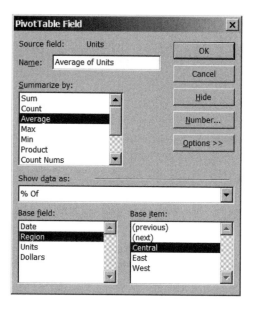

Figure 3-9. *The custom calculation % Of, with Region as a base field*

The column for the Central shows 100%, because it's being compared to itself. The remaining columns show the percent of their average units per sale, compared to the Central region's average units per sale.

3.6. Using Custom Calculations: % Difference From

Problem

You have monthly sales figures and forecasts for each product, and would like to compare actual sales to forecast sales for each product per month.

In your pivot table, Date (grouped by Month) and Product are in the row area, Status (Actual or Forecast) is in the column area, and Units sold (Sum of Units) is in the data area (see Figure 3-10).

Solution

Use % Difference From to compare the Actual to Forecast items in the Status field.

Tip Leave the original copy of the Sum of Units field, so you can see the Units quantity, as well as the % Difference From calculation.

---

1. Add another copy of the Units field to the data area.

2. Right-click on the Sum of Units2 heading, and choose Field Settings.

3. Click the Options button.

4. From the dropdown list for Show data as, select % Difference From.

5. For the Base field, select Status.

6. For the Base item, select Forecast, and then click the OK button.

		Data ▼	Status ▼		
		Sum of Units		% Diff	
Date ▼	Product ▼	Forecast	Actual	Forecast	Actual
Jan	A703	967	823		-15%
	B306	702	398		-43%
	C589	886	1299		47%
	D726	405	93		-77%
Jan Total		2960	2613		-12%

Figure 3-10. *The % Difference calculation from the forecast in units sold per product per month*

The Forecast column will be empty, because it won't be compared to itself. The Actual column shows the % Difference From calculation from the forecast in units sold.

Tip Select the cell that contains the Sum of Units2 label, and type a more descriptive name, for example, **% Diff**.

3.7. Using Custom Calculations: Running Total

Problem

You have monthly sales figures for each product, and would like to see a running total by month. In your pivot table, Date (grouped by Month) is in the row area, Product is in the column area, and Units sold (Sum of Units) is in the data area (see the table at the left in Figure 3-11).

Solution

Use a running total in a custom calculation to accumulate the sales amounts per product, down through the list of months.

1. Right-click on the Sum of Total button, and choose Field Settings.

2. Click the Options button.

3. From the dropdown list for Show data as, select Running Total In.

4. For the Base field, select Date, then click the OK button.

Caution If you select a base field that isn't in the row or column area, all the results will show an #N/A error. Also, if there's an error in any month's results, it will carry down through the remaining months.

No Custom Calculation				Running Total in Date				Running Total in Product			
Sum of Units				Sum of Units				Sum of Units			
Date ▼	A703	B306	Grand Total	Date ▼	A703	B306	Grand Total	Date ▼	A703	B306	Grand Total
Jan	295	398	693	Jan	295	398	693	Jan	295	693	
Feb	326	19	345	Feb	621	417	1038	Feb	326	345	
Mar	120	197	317	Mar	741	614	1355	Mar	120	317	
Grand Total	741	614	1355	Grand Total				Grand Total	741	1355	

Figure 3-11. *Running total in a custom calculation with different base fields*

How It Works

With Date as the base field, each Product column shows a running total for the year, by month (see the center table in Figure 3-11). If you select Product as the base field, the running total accumulates across the pivot table, in each month row (see the right table in Figure 3-11).

For pivot tables with multiple fields in the row area, the running totals work the same way, but may be harder to follow as the layout becomes more complex. Using the previous example, with Product moved to the row area, the running total amounts are the same but are arranged vertically (see Figure 3-12).

No Custom Calculation			Running Total in Date			Running Total in Product		
Sum of Units			Sum of Units			Sum of Units		
Date ▼	Prod ▼	Total	Date ▼	Prod ▼	Total	Date ▼	Prod ▼	Total
Jan	A703	295	Jan	A703	295	Jan	A703	295
	B306	398		B306	398		B306	693
Jan Total		693	Jan Total		693	Jan Total		
Feb	A703	326	Feb	A703	621	Feb	A703	326
	B306	19		B306	417		B306	345
Feb Total		345	Feb Total		1038	Feb Total		
Mar	A703	120	Mar	A703	741	Mar	A703	120
	B306	197		B306	614		B306	317
Mar Total		317	Mar Total		1355	Mar Total		
Grand Total		1355	Grand Total			Grand Total		

Figure 3-12. *Running total in a custom calculation with different base fields and two row fields*

3.8. Using Custom Calculations: % of Row

Problem

You have monthly sales figures for each sales manager, and would like to see what percent of their total sales came from each product category. In your pivot table, Sales Manager is in the row area, Category is in the column area, and Units is in the data area (see the table at the left in Figure 3-13).

Solution

Use the % of Row custom calculation to show the percent per category for each Sales Manager's sales.

1. Right-click on the Sum of Sales button, and choose Field Settings.

2. Click the Options button.

3. From the dropdown list for Show data as, select % of row, then click OK.

Note There's no option to select a base field or base item with this custom calculation.

In the row for each Sales Manager, you can see the percent of the total that was sold in each category (see the table at the right in Figure 3-13).

Units Sold (Thousands)

Sum of Units	Cate ▼			
SalesMgr ▼	Bars	Cookies	Crackers	Grand Total
Boston	23	29	29	82
Lee	16	23	23	62
Parent	22	25	31	78
Grand Total	61	77	83	221

Units Sold (% of Row)

Sum of Units	Cate ▼			
SalesMgr ▼	Bars	Cookies	Crackers	Grand Total
Boston	28%	36%	36%	100%
Lee	27%	37%	37%	100%
Parent	28%	32%	40%	100%
Grand Total	28%	35%	37%	100%

Figure 3-13. *The % of Row custom calculation shows category sales percentages.*

Tip You can hide the Grand Total for Rows, because it will always equal 100%.

3.9. Using Custom Calculations: % of Column

Problem

You have monthly sales figures for each product category, and would like to see what per-cent of their total sales were attributed to each sales manager. In your pivot table, Sales Manager is in the row area, Category is in the column area, and Units is in the data area (see the table at the left in Figure 3-14).

Solution

1. Right-click on the Sum of Units Count button, and choose Field Settings.

2. Click the Options button.

3. From the dropdown list for Show data as, select % of column, then click OK.

In the column for each Category, you can see the percent of the total for each Sales Manager (see the table at the right in Figure 3-14).

Units Sold (Thousands)					Units Sold (% of Column)				
Sum of Unit Ca ▼					Sum of Units Cate ▼				
SalesMgr ▼	Bars	Cookies	Crackers	Grand Total	SalesMgr ▼	Bars	Cookies	Crackers	Grand Total
Boston	23	29	29	82	Boston	38%	38%	36%	37%
Lee	16	23	23	62	Lee	27%	29%	27%	28%
Parent	22	25	31	78	Parent	36%	32%	37%	35%
Grand Total	61	77	83	221	Grand Total	100%	100%	100%	100%

Figure 3-14. *The % of Column custom calculation shows Sales Manager percentages.*

Tip There's no % of Subtotal custom calculation available in a pivot table, but you can arrange fields in the row and column areas, then use % of Row or % or Column to show the percentages.

3.10. Using Custom Calculations: % of Total

Problem

You have monthly insurance policy counts for your regional offices. You'd like to see what percentage of the existing policies are in each region, for auto policies and property policies.

In your pivot table, Region is in the row area, Policy Type is in the column area, and Sum of Policies is in the data area. Policy Status is in the page area, and Existing has been selected (see the table at the left in Figure 3-15).

Solution

1. Right-click on the Sum of Policies button, and choose Field Settings.

2. Click the Options button.

3. From the dropdown list for Show data as, select % of total, then click OK.

In each cell, you can see the percent of the total that was sold in each region for each policy type (see the table at the right in Figure 3-15).

Policies (Thousands)				Policies (% of Total)			
Status	Existing ▼			Status	Existing ▼		
Sum of Policies	InsTyp ▼			Sum of Policies	InsTyp ▼		
Region ▼	Auto	Prop	Grand Total	Region ▼	Auto	Prop	Grand Total
Central	36	35	71	Central	20%	19%	39%
East	26	22	48	East	14%	12%	26%
West	33	31	64	West	18%	17%	35%
Grand Total	94	89	183	Grand Total	52%	48%	100%

Figure 3-15. *The % of Total custom calculation shows percentage policy type by Region.*

3.11. Using Custom Calculations: Index

Problem

You have monthly insurance policy counts for your regional offices. You'd like to compare canceled policies in each region, for both auto policies and property policies. In your pivot table, Region is in the row area, Policy Type is in the column area, and Sum of Policies is in the data area. Policy Status is in the page area, and Cancel has been selected (see the table at the left in Figure 3-16).

Solution

Use the Index option to show the relative weight of each cell when compared to its row total, its column total, and the grand total.

1. Right-click on the Sum of Total button, and choose Field Settings.

2. Click the Options button.

3. From the dropdown list for Show data as, select Index, then click OK.

In each cell, you can see its index (see the table at the right in Figure 3-16).

Policies (Thousands)				
Status	Cancel ▼			
Sum of Policies	InsTyp ▼			
				Grand
Region ▼		Auto	Prop	Total
Central		9.8	10.5	20.3
East		5.6	6.9	12.5
West		10.5	10.8	21.3
Grand Total		25.9	28.2	54.1

Policies (Index)				
Status	Cancel ▼			
Sum of Policies	InsTy ▼			
				Grand
Region ▼		Auto	Prop	Total
Central		101%	99%	100%
East		94%	106%	100%
West		103%	97%	100%
Grand Total		100%	100%	100%

Figure 3-16. *The Index custom calculation shows an index of the canceled policy type by Region.*

How It Works

The index formula is

```
((value in cell) x (Grand Total of Grand Totals)) /
((Grand Row Total) x (Grand Column Total))
```

Two cells with the same number of canceled policies may have a different index. A value of 1000 will have a higher index if it's the highest value in its row and column, but the same value would have a lower index if it's the lowest value in its row and column.

3.12. Using Formulas: Calculated Field vs. Calculated Item

In addition to the built-in summary functions and custom calculations, you can write your own formulas in a pivot table to create calculated fields and calculated items.

■**Note** Formulas are available only in non-OLAP based pivot tables.

Problem

You're not sure when to use a calculated field and when to use a calculated item.

Solution

You can create calculated items in a field to perform calculations on other items in that field. For example, if your pivot table contains a Status field that stores the Order status, you could create a Sold item that sums the items with a status of Shipped, Pending, and Backorder but doesn't include Canceled.

You can create calculated fields to perform calculations on other fields in the pivot table. For example, you may have agreed to pay sales representatives a 3 percent bonus on any products for which they sold more than 100 units. The calculated field would display the bonus amount using values in the Units and Total fields.

▓**Caution** If you create a calculated item or a calculated field, you may not be able to move the pivot field to the page area.

How It Works

A calculated item becomes an item in a pivot field. Its calculation can use the contents of other items in the same field. A calculated field becomes a new field in the pivot table, and its calculation can use the contents of other fields.

Calculated items and calculated fields are calculated differently. For calculated items, the individual records in the source data are calculated, then the results are summed. For example, if you create a Tax field that multiplies the items by 7 percent, the value in each record is multiplied by 7 percent, then the individual tax amounts are summed for the Grand Total.

For calculated fields, the individual amounts are summed, then the calculation is performed on the total amount.

▓**Note** You can't create formulas that refer to the pivot table totals or subtotals. Also, the calculated item and calculated field formulas can't refer to worksheet cells by address or by name.

3.13. Using Formulas: Adding Items with a Calculated Item

Problem

Your pivot table contains an Order Status field, and you'd like to create a Sold item that sums the items with a status of Shipped, Pending, and Backorder but doesn't include Canceled.

Solution

Create a calculated item that adds the Shipped, Pending, and Backorder items.

1. In the pivot table, select the Status field button.

2. On the Pivot toolbar, choose PivotTable ➤ Formulas ➤ Calculated Item.

3. Type a name for the Calculated Item, for example, **Sold**.

4. Press the Tab key to move to the Formula box.

5. In the Fields list, ensure that Status is selected.

6. In the Items list, double-click on Shipped, then type a plus sign (+).

7. Double-click on Pending, and type a plus sign, then double-click on Backorder.

8. The complete formula is

   ```
   =Shipped+ Pending+ Backorder
   ```

9. Click the OK button to save the calculated item, and close the dialog box.

10. In the pivot table, hide the Shipped, Pending, and Backorder items to see the correct Grand Totals.

3.14. Using Formulas: Modifying a Calculated Item

Problem

After you create a calculated item, you want to change it.

Solution

You can go back into the Formula dialog box, and modify the calculated item.

1. In the pivot table, select the field button for the field that contains the calculated item.

2. On the Pivot toolbar, choose PivotTable ➤ Formulas ➤ Calculated Item.

3. From the Name dropdown, select the name of the calculated item that you want to modify.

4. In the Formula box, change the formula.

5. Click the Modify button.

6. Click OK to close the dialog box.

3.15. Using Formulas: Temporarily Removing a Calculated Item

Problem

After you create a calculated item, you want to temporarily remove it from the pivot table.

Solution

You can hide a calculated item, then show it again later.

1. Click the dropdown arrow in the calculated item's field list.

2. Remove the checkmark from the calculated item.

3. Click OK.

3.16. Using Formulas: Permanently Removing a Calculated Item

Problem

After you create a calculated item, you want to permanently remove it from the pivot table.

Solution

1. In the pivot table, select the field button for the field that contains the calculated item.

2. On the Pivot toolbar, choose PivotTable ➤ Formulas ➤ Calculated Item.

3. From the Name dropdown, select the name of the calculated item that you want to delete.

4. Click the Delete button.

5. Click OK to close the dialog box.

3.17. Using Formulas: Using Index Numbers in a Calculated Item

Problem

The items in your field change frequently, and you'd like to refer to the items by number in the formulas instead of by name.

Solution

You can use an index number to refer to field items. For example, to multiply the data for the first item in the Date field by 5 percent, use the following formula:

```
=Date[1]*.05
```

■**Caution** If you create a calculated item that refers to items by position, the Top 10 AutoShow and AutoSort options become unavailable, and are reset to Manual or Off.

3.18. Using Formulas: Using Relative Position Numbers in a Calculated Item

Problem

You'd like to refer to items by their position relative to the calculated item instead of by name.

Solution

You can refer to items by their position relative to the calculated item. For example, to calculate the difference between the data for the first visible Date item and the last visible Date item, use the following formula:

```
=Date[1]-Date[-1]
```

This formula assumes that the calculated item will be last in its field and the last date is directly above it (see Figure 3-17).

Subtotal	Region ▾			
Date ▾	East	West	Central	Grand Total
2/1/2006	284	250	108	641
2/6/2006	299	302		602
2/11/2006		320	269	589
2/16/2006	299	550	147	997
2/21/2006	420		269	689
2/26/2006	105	404	75	584
DiffFirstLast	**179**	**-155**	**33**	**58**

Figure 3-17. *The DiffFirstLast calculated item refers to the dates by index number.*

■**Caution** If you create a calculated item that refers to items by relative position, the Top 10 AutoShow and AutoSort options become unavailable, and are reset to Manual or Off.

3.19. Using Formulas: Modifying a Calculated Item Formula in a Cell

Problem

You'd like a calculated item to be slightly different for one column.

Solution

You can select a cell that shows the result of a calculated item, and modify its formula in the formula bar. For example, in the previous calculated item example, the index number was used to calculate the difference between the first visible item and the last:

```
=Date[1]-Date[-1]
```

If one of the columns has a blank cell in the first position, you can modify the formula to refer to the second item:

```
=Date[2]-Date[-1]
```

■**Caution** The Undo feature is not available after making this change.

To make the change, select the cell, and modify the formula in the formula bar.

> **Tip** Unlike worksheet formulas, where you can select several cells, make a change, then press Ctrl + Enter to apply the change to all selected cells, the pivot table cells with calculated item formulas must be changed individually.

3.20. Using Formulas: Creating a Calculated Field

Problem

Your pivot table contains a Total field that stores the total amount of each sale, and a Units field, that stores the number of units sold. You'd like a Bonus field that calculates the bonus payable if a sales representative has sold more than 100 units of any product.

Solution

1. In the pivot table, select any cell.

2. On the Pivot toolbar, choose PivotTable ➤ Formulas ➤ Calculated Field.

3. Type a name for the calculated field, for example, **Bonus**.

4. Press the Tab key to move to the Formula box.

5. Type the formula

   ```
   =IF(Units>100,Total*0.03,0)
   ```

6. Click the OK button to save the calculated field and close the dialog box.

> **Note** You can't change the summary function for a calculated field. Sum is the only function available for these fields.

3.21. Using Formulas: Modifying a Calculated Field

Problem

After you create a calculated field, you'd like to change it.

Solution

You can go back into the Formula dialog box, and modify the settings.

1. In the pivot table, select any cell.

2. On the Pivot toolbar, choose PivotTable ➤ Formulas ➤ Calculated Field.

3. From the Name dropdown, select the name of the calculated field that you want to modify.

4. In the Formula box, change the formula.

5. Click the Modify button, then click OK to close the dialog box.

3.22. Using Formulas: Temporarily Removing a Calculated Field

Problem

After you create a calculated field, you'd like to remove it from the pivot table temporarily.

Solution

You can hide a calculated field, then show it again later:

1. Click the dropdown arrow in the Data field list.

2. Remove the checkmark from the calculated field, then click OK.

3.23. Using Formulas: Permanently Removing a Calculated Field

Problem

After you create a calculated field, you'd like to remove it from the pivot table permanently.

Solution

1. In the pivot table, select any cell.

2. On the Pivot toolbar, choose PivotTable ➤ Formulas ➤ Calculated Field.

3. From the Name dropdown, select the name of the calculated field that you want to delete.

4. Click the Delete button, then click OK to close the dialog box.

3.24. Using Formulas: Determining the Type of Formula

Problem

You can't tell if a formula is a calculated item or calculated field.

Solution

If it's a calculated field, you'll see its name in the PivotTable Field List. If the name doesn't appear there, it's a calculated item.

3.25. Using Formulas: Adding a Calculated Item to a Field With Grouped Items

Problem

You want to add a calculated item in a field, but some items are grouped, and you get an error message.

Solution

Ungroup the items and create the calculated item. Then, regroup the items in the field.

3.26. Using Formulas: Calculating the Difference Between Plan and Actual

Problem

In your pivot table you have a Plan amount and an Actual amount. You'd like to calculate the percent difference between Actual and Plan.

Solution

If Plan and Actual are separate fields in the source data, you can create a calculated field to calculate the percent difference. If they're items in the same field, use the % Difference From custom calculation.

3.27. Using Formulas: Correcting the Grand Total for a Calculated Field

Problem

You have a calculated field that calculates a customer discount based on each month's orders:

```
=IF(Units >1000,Dollars *-0.02,0)
```

You assumed the grand total would be a sum of the discount amounts, but it performs the same discount calculation in the grand total row, creating the wrong total (see Figure 3-18).

Solution

The grand total for a calculated field will perform the same calculation that's defined in the calculated field. As a workaround, you could use a GetPivotData formula outside the pivot table to extract the line totals, and then sum those amounts (see Figure 3-18).

MonthNo ▼	Data ▼ Units	Dollars	Discount		Discounts	
1	1,029	1,683	$ (33.66)	1	$ (33.66)	
2	987	1,502	$ -	2	$ -	
3	1,129	1,862	$ (37.23)	3	$ (37.23)	
Grand Total	3,145	5,047	$(100.93)		$ (70.89)	

Figure 3-18. *The Grand Total is incorrect for the calculated field.*

3.28. Using Formulas: Counting Unique Items in a Calculated Field

Problem

In your pivot table, you want a count of unique customers who placed orders, but the data area will only show a count of orders. Some customers placed several orders, so the count of orders doesn't tell you how many customers you have.

Solution

A pivot table won't calculate a unique count. You could add a column to the source data, then add that field to the pivot table. For example, to count unique customers in column A, use the following formula:

```
=IF(COUNTIF($A$1:A2,A2)=1,1,0)
```

Copy this formula down to all rows in the list, then add the field to the pivot table data area using the Sum function.

How It Works

The COUNTIF formula checks the range A1:A2, and counts the instances of the customer name that's entered in cell A2.

For the first occurrence of the name, the count is one. The IF formula checks the result of the COUNTIF formula, and if the count is one, the IF formula returns a one.

For the next occurrence of the customer name, the COUNTIF formula would return a 2, and the IF formula would return a zero.

When you copy the formula down the column on the worksheet, only the first occurrence of each customer name returns a one, so the sum of this column is the number of unique customers.

3.29. Using Formulas: Correcting Results in a Calculated Field

Problem

In your source data, you have columns for price and quantity, but the results are incorrect when you use a calculated field to multiply price by quantity.

Solution

If you use a calculated field to create the totals in the pivot table, you may get incorrect results. For example, the pivot table may show the Sum of Price multiplied by Sum of Quantity for results that are much too high. Instead, calculate the total sales (price × quantity) for each row in the source data table. Then, add that field to the pivot table's data area to get the correct totals.

3.30. Using Formulas: Listing All Formulas

Problem

You're documenting your workbook, and you would like to create a list of all the formulas that you created in the pivot table.

Solution

1. Select any cell in the pivot table.

2. From the Pivot toolbar, choose PivotTable ➤ Formulas ➤ List Formulas.

A new sheet is inserted in the workbook, with a list of calculated items and a list of calculated fields.

3.31. Using Formulas: Accidentally Creating a Calculated Item

Problem

Your pivot table contains a calculated item, but you didn't create one and aren't sure how it got there.

Solution

It's possible to accidentally create a calculated formula if you drag the fill handle on one of the labels. Follow these steps to remove the formula:

1. Select the field button for the field that contains the calculated item.

2. From the Pivot toolbar, choose PivotTable ➤ Formulas ➤ Calculated Item.

3. From the dropdown list of formulas, select the formula you want to delete.

4. Click the Delete button, then click the Close button.

3.32. Using Formulas: Solve Order

Problem

In your pivot table, there are two calculated items:

```
CancelRate: = Cancel/( Cancel+ Existing)
All: East + West
```

In the pivot table, grand totals are hidden and the calculated items are shown (see the table at the left in Figure 3-19).

Original Solve Order			
Sum of Polic Regi ▼			
Status ▼	East	West	All
Cancel	1.6	1.6	3.2
Existing	47.6	63.8	111.5
CancelRate	3.3%	2.5%	**5.8%**

Solve Order Changed			
Sum of Polic Regi ▼			
Status ▼	East	West	All
Cancel	1.6	1.6	3.2
Existing	47.6	63.8	111.5
CancelRate	3.3%	2.5%	**2.8%**

Figure 3-19. *The pivot table, with two calculated items*

However, the CancelRate for All is incorrect. It's a sum of the CancelRate for the individual regions, instead of a calculation of the CancelRate, based on the All totals.

You'd prefer to have the CancelRate for All be calculated like the CancelRate for the individual regions.

Solution

You can change the Solve Order for the calculated items to get the result that you want:

1. Select a cell in the pivot table.

2. From the Pivot toolbar, choose PivotTable ➤ Formulas ➤ Solve Order.

3. Select the All formula, and click the Move Up button.

The All CancelRate is adjusted, and shows the All cancel ratio, instead of the sum of region ratios (see the table at the right in Figure 3-19).

■**Note** When you change the Solve Order, it affects all calculated items in the pivot table.

How It Works

Calculated items are added to the Solve Order list in the order in which they're created. For any result that is affected by two or more calculated items, the last calculation listed is the one that determines its value.

In this example, the CancelRate calculated item was created first, then the All calculated item. The bottom-right cell in the pivot table is affected by both calculated items.

In the original Solve Order, the All calculated item is last in the Solve Order, so the bottom-right cell shows the result of that formula: East + West.

In the revised Solve Order, the CancelRate calculated item is last in the Solve Order, so the bottom-right cell shows the result of that formula: Cancel/(Cancel+ Existing).

CHAPTER 4

■■■

Formatting a Pivot Table

Common problems with pivot table formatting include loss of formatting when the pivot table is changed or refreshed, showing or hiding subtotals and grand totals, and retaining formats applied in the source data. The solutions in this chapter are those that can be applied manually. Some formatting issues should be addressed by using macros, and are included in Chapter 13.

4.1. Using AutoFormat: Applying a Predefined Format

Problem

You'd like a quick way to format your pivot table.

Solution

You can use the AutoFormat command to apply a predefined format.

1. Select a cell in the pivot table.

2. Choose Format ➤ AutoFormat.

3. Select one of the AutoFormats, and then click OK.

How It Works

When you select one of the PivotTable AutoFormats, it will apply specific cell formatting to different parts of the pivot table. For example, all of the row subtotals may be changed to bold Arial font, with yellow fill color in the cell. When you pivot the fields, the formatting is retained.

Many of the AutoFormats change the layout of the pivot table, moving row or column fields to a different area. Some add blank rows between items. Number formatting and date formatting may be changed.

Note You can't create your own AutoFormats, or modify the existing AutoFormats.

4.2. Using AutoFormat: Removing an AutoFormat

Problem

You applied an AutoFormat to a pivot table, and would like to remove it.

Solution

To remove an AutoFormat immediately after applying it, you can click the Undo button, or choose Edit ➤ Undo AutoFormat, or press Ctrl+Z on the keyboard.

To remove an AutoFormat later, choose Format ➤ AutoFormat. From the list of Auto-Formats, select PivotTable Classic or None, and then click OK.

How It Works

Applying the PivotTable Classic AutoFormat or selecting None will remove the cell fill colors and other formatting options that were applied by previous AutoFormats or manually applied to the cells. Number formats that were applied as a field setting will not be removed.

4.3. Using AutoFormat: Applying a Standard Table AutoFormat

You'd like to apply one of the standard table AutoFormats, but it isn't available when you're formatting a pivot table.

Solution

Some AutoFormats aren't listed when you apply AutoFormats to a pivot table. A different list of AutoFormats is available if you're formatting a regular table. Follow these steps to use one of the standard AutoFormats:

1. Select a cell in a normal worksheet table (for example, select a cell in your source data table).

2. Choose Format ➤ AutoFormat.

3. Select one of the AutoFormats, and then click OK.

4. Select a cell in the pivot table.

5. Press the F4 key to repeat the previous formatting.

4.4. Using the Enable Selection Option

Problem

You want to select and format all the row subtotals for the Region field at the same time, instead of formatting each one separately.

Solution

You can select them all, and then format them together. To select them, you may have to activate the Enable Selection option:

1. Select a cell in the pivot table, and from the PivotTable toolbar, choose PivotTable ➤ Select.

2. If Enable Selection is not activated, click it to activate the feature (see Figure 4-1).

Figure 4-1. *The Enable Selection option turned on*

3. Point to the left side of a cell that contains a subtotal label, and when the pointer changes to a black arrow shape (see Figure 4-2), click to select all the subtotals for that field.

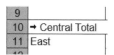

Figure 4-2. *The black arrow pointer at the left of the subtotal in Row 10*

4. Format the selected subtotals.

4.5. Losing Formatting When Refreshing the Pivot Table

Problem

Your pivot table formatting is lost when you refresh or change the pivot table.

Solution

Some formatting loss can be prevented if you change the Formatting options in the PivotTable Options dialog box:

1. Right-click a cell in the pivot table.

2. Choose Table Options.

3. Under Format options, remove the checkmark from AutoFormat table.

4. Add a checkmark to Preserve formatting, and then click OK.

Then, when you apply formatting, do the following:

1. Ensure that Enable Selection is turned on (see Figure 4-1).

2. Use the pivot table selection feature to select the elements that you want to format (point to the top or left edge of the element, and click when the black arrow appears) (see Figure 4-2).

To prevent loss of number formatting, apply formatting to the field instead of selected cells:

1. Right-click the field button or Field heading cell, and choose Field Settings.

2. Click the Number button, and select the number formatting option you want.

3. Click OK to close the Format Cells dialog box, and click OK to close the PivotTable Field dialog box.

4.6. Retaining the Source Data Formatting

Problem

The numbers in your source data are formatted as currency, with no decimals, and a dollar sign. When you add the field to the pivot table's data area, the formatting is lost.

Solution

Although source data number formatting is generally maintained if you add a field to the row, column, or page area, it's lost if you add the field to the data area. To make it easier to reapply the formatting in the pivot table, you can create a style with all the format settings.

■**Tip** Styles are available in regular worksheet cells too, so you can apply them within a PivotTable report or in other cells.

---

1. Select a cell in the source data that has the format you want to save as a style.

2. Choose Format ➤ Style.

3. Type a name for your new style, for example, **CURR NO DEC**.

■**Tip** It will be easier to identify your styles if you type them in all capitals.

---

4. Remove the checkmark from any features you don't want included in the style. In this style, you may want only the number formatting and thus you should remove all the other checkmarks.

5. If you want to change any of the format settings, click the Modify button, adjust the settings, and click OK in the Format Cells dialog box.

6. Click OK to close the Style dialog box and save the style.

Follow these steps to apply a style:

1. Select the cells where you want to apply the style.

2. Choose Format ➤ Style.

3. Select a style from the dropdown list, and click the OK button.

If you use styles frequently, you can add the Style dropdown to one of your toolbars:

1. Choose Tools ➤ Customize.

2. On the Commands tab, select the Format Category.

3. Drag the Style dropdown to one of your existing toolbars, and click the Close button.

4.7. Hiding Data Errors on Worksheet

Problem

There are errors in the pivot table data, and you'd like to hide them on the worksheet.

Solution

By default, error values are displayed in a pivot table. You can hide the errors by changing the pivot table options:

1. Right-click a cell in the pivot table.

2. Choose Table Options.

3. To turn on the For error values, show option, add a checkmark in the check box.

4. Leave the text box blank, and the errors will be replaced with blank cells.

■**Note** This setting only affects cells in the data area of the pivot table. If there are error values in the source data that appear in the row, column, or page area, they will not be replaced.

4.8. Hiding Errors When Printing

Problem

There are errors in the pivot table data, and you'd like to hide them when printing the worksheet.

Solution

You can hide the errors in the printed copy by changing the page setup options:

1. Choose File ➤ Page Setup.

2. On the Sheet tab in the Print section, select <blank> from the Cell errors as dropdown.

4.9. Showing Zero in Empty Data Cells

Problem

Some cells in the data area are empty, and you'd prefer that they contain a zero.

Solution

Change the pivot table options:

1. Right-click a cell in the pivot table, and choose Table Options.

2. Add a checkmark to For empty cells, show, and in the text box, type a zero (see Figure 4-3).

3. Click OK.

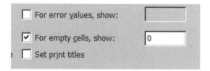

Figure 4-3. *Set empty data cells to display a zero.*

4.10. Using Conditional Formatting in a Pivot Table

Problem

You want to use conditional formatting to highlight the high and low values in your pivot table data. Values below 25 should have a red background, and values above 75 should have a green background.

Solution

You can apply conditional formatting in a pivot table, just as you would on normal worksheet cells (Format ➤ Conditional Formatting). However, if the pivot fields are rearranged, the conditional formatting doesn't move with them but stays on the cells that were originally formatted. If your pivot table is fairly static in size and shape, you may be able to use conditional formatting without too many problems. If your pivot table layout changes frequently, you'll need to remove and reapply the conditional formatting each time.

Another option is to use a custom number format to apply font color to a cell that meets specific criteria, and the format will move with the cell if the pivot table is rearranged. For example, to change the font color to red if the cell value is less than 25, follow these steps:

1. Right-click a cell in the field that you want to format, and choose Field Settings.

2. In the PivotTable Field dialog box, click the Number button.

3. In the Category list, select Custom.

4. In the Type box, type the format

   `[Red][<25]General;General`

5. Click OK to close the Format Cells dialog box, and click OK to close the PivotTable Field dialog box.

How It Works

Eight different colors are available for custom number formats, and you can specify conditions under which to apply a color. For details and a list of available colors, see the "Guidelines for custom number formats" topic in Excel's Help.

4.11. Creating Custom Number Formats in the Source Data

Problem

Some numbers in your data have a less than sign—for example, <0.1—and they aren't showing up in the pivot table.

Solution

If the less than and greater than operators are typed in the source data, they change the numbers into text. In the pivot table, text is displayed as zero in the data area.

You could use a custom number format in the source data instead of typed operators, and the values would display correctly in the pivot table.

1. In the source data, select the cells that you want to format, and choose Format ➤ Cells.

2. On the Number tab, select the Custom category.

3. In the Type box, type **[<0.1]"<0.1";General**.

4. Click OK.

4.12. Totaling Hours in a Time Field

Problem

In your source data, you record the time spent on projects per employee per day. In the pivot table, you want the total time per project, but the results are shown as time rather than total time. For example, the sum of 10:00 +10:00 + 5:00 is shown as 1:00 instead of 25:00.

Solution

In the pivot table, format the cells that contain total times with the custom number format [h]:mm, and they'll total correctly.

4.13. Displaying Hundredths of Seconds in a Pivot Table

Problem

In your source data there are times, with a custom format of m:ss.00. The times show correctly in the worksheet—for example, 5:15.25—but are rounded in the pivot table, with all the hundredths showing as zero—for example, 5:15.00.

Solution

1. In the source data, add a column with a formula that refers to the time column—for example, =B2.

2. Format this column as General instead of Time.

3. Add this new field to the pivot table, and format it with the custom number format of m:ss.00.

4.14. Centering Field Labels Vertically

Problem

You'd like to center the field labels vertically for the outer fields in the row area of the pivot table.

Solution

1. Right-click a cell in the pivot table, and choose Table Options.

2. Under Format options, add a checkmark to Merge labels.

3. Click OK.

This setting will automatically center the labels vertically and horizontally.

4.15. Applying an Indented AutoFormat

Problem

You'd like to format the pivot table in a traditional report outline layout, with headings down the side and the data in columns.

Solution

1. Select a cell in the pivot table, and choose Format ➤ AutoFormat.

2. In the AutoFormat dialog box, select one of the Report AutoFormats, and the pivot table fields will be rearranged automatically. Column fields will move to the outer row area, and the data will be in columns (see Figure 4-4).

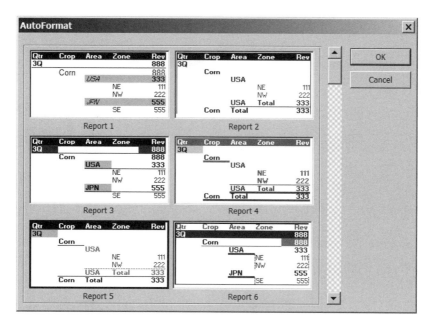

Figure 4-4. *Report options in the AutoFormat dialog box*

■**Note** This type of layout is called *Outline form* in the PivotTable Field Layout dialog box.

4.16. Creating an Indented Format

Problem

You'd like to format the pivot table in a traditional report outline layout, with headings down the side and the data in columns. You don't want to use one of the built-in AutoFormats, because you want to maintain the current fonts and fill colors in the pivot table.

Solution

You can manually create an indented format, similar to those created by the Report AutoFormats.

1. Move all the heading fields to the row area of the pivot table.

2. Double-click the field button for the outermost row field.

3. In the PivotTable Field dialog box, click the Layout button.

    4. For Display Options, select Show items in outline form, then click OK.

    5. Click OK to close the PivotTable Field dialog box.

How It Works

When you set the outer fields to indented, it simulates the look of a traditional report by placing each outer field item on one row, with its items in rows below. You can apply the outline form option to all but the innermost row fields.

    To enhance the traditional appearance, you can show the totals at the top of each item, or leave them at the bottom. For more visual separation between items, you can select to add blank rows between items.

4.17. Applying a Tabular AutoFormat

Problem

You'd like to format the pivot table in a tabular layout, with headings down the side and across the top, with the data in the intersections.

Solution

    1. Select a cell in the pivot table, and choose Format ➤ AutoFormat.

    2. Apply one of the Table AutoFormats to the pivot table, and the fields may be rearranged automatically. If there are no column fields, the outer row fields will move to the column area, and the data will be in columns (see Figure 4-5).

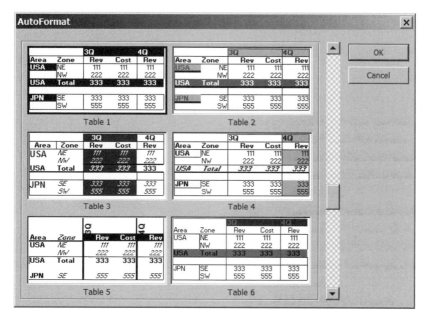

Figure 4-5. *Table options in the AutoFormat dialog box*

■Note This type of layout is called *Tabular form* in the PivotTable Field Layout dialog box.

4.18. Displaying Subtotals at the Top of a Group

Problem

In your pivot table, you'd like the subtotals to appear at the top of the row field items.

Solution

If the pivot table is in outline (Report) layout, you can format the field to control where its subtotals appear:

1. Double-click the field button to open the PivotTable Field dialog box.

2. Click the Layout button.

3. Select Show items in outline form and add a checkmark to Display subtotals at top of group.

4. Click OK, then click OK to close the PivotTable Field dialog box.

4.19. Separating Field Items with Blank Rows

Problem

To make the pivot table easier to read, you'd like each row field item to be followed by a blank row.

Solution

In both outline (Report) layout and Crosstab (tabular) layout, you can format an outer row field so each item has a blank row after it:

1. Double-click the field button to open the PivotTable Field dialog box.

2. Click the Layout button.

3. Add a checkmark to Insert blank line after each item.

4. Click OK, then click OK to close the PivotTable Field dialog box.

▇Tip You can't enter text in the blank row, but you can format the row—for example, add a fill color to visually separate the items.

4.20. Turning Off Subtotals

Problem

When you add more fields to the row or column area, some of the fields get subtotals. You'd like to stop them from appearing.

Solution

There's no setting you can change to stop the subtotals from automatically appearing for outer row and column fields. However, you can turn them off once they appear:

1. Double-click the field button.

2. For Subtotals, select None, then click OK.

4.21. Repeating Row Headings

Problem

The row headings only appear in the first row for each group. You would like them to appear in each row.

Solution

The row headings show once in a pivot table, and there's no setting you can change to force them to repeat. If you need to print a copy of the pivot table with a heading in each row, you can make a copy of the pivot table and repeat the headings there:

1. Select a cell in the pivot table, and on the PivotTable toolbar, choose PivotTable ➤ Select ➤ Entire Table.

2. On the Standard toolbar, click the Copy button, then select a cell where you want to paste the copy.

3. On the Standard toolbar, choose Edit ➤ Paste Special, select Values, and click OK.

4. If you want to retain the formatting, choose Edit ➤ Paste Special, select Formats, and click OK.

5. In the copied pivot table, select the column that contains the row field headings.

6. Choose Edit ➤ Go To, and click the Special button.

7. Select Blanks, then click OK.

8. Type an equal sign, then press the Up arrow on the keyboard—this will enter a reference to the cell above.

9. Press Ctrl+Enter—this enters the formula in all selected cells.

If you plan to sort or filter the data, the formulas must be changed to values:

1. Select the entire column that contains the row headings, and copy it.

2. With the column still selected, choose Edit ➤ Paste Special.

3. Select Values, then click OK.

▓**Caution** Use Paste Special Values with caution if there are other cells in the range that contain formulas.

4.22. Retaining Formatting for Temporarily Removed Fields

Problem

You formatted a row field with a custom number format, then temporarily removed it from the PivotTable report. When you dragged it back to the pivot table, the custom format was lost, and you had to reapply it.

Solution

Instead of removing fields from the pivot table, drag them to the page area temporarily. They'll retain their formatting, and you can move them back to their original position when required.

4.23. Applying Formatting with the Format Painter

Problem

If you use the Format Painter (see Figure 4-6) to copy a format from a cell, you can't use the pivot table selection feature to apply the copied format to part of the pivot table. You can only drag over cells to apply the format.

Figure 4-6. *The Format Painter button copies formats from the selected range.*

Note The Format Painter button on the Formatting toolbar copies formats from one range of cells, and pastes it to another range of cells.

Solution

You can't use the Format Painter, but you could add the Paste Formatting button to one of your existing toolbars, and use it to apply the formatting.

To add the Paste Formatting button to a toolbar, follow these steps:

1. On the Excel worksheet menu bar, choose Tools ➤ Customize.

2. On the Commands tab, under Categories, select Edit.

3. In the list of Commands, locate Paste Formatting, and drag it to one of your toolbars.

4. Click the Close button to close the Customize dialog box.

To use the Paste Formatting button to apply formatting, follow these steps:

1. Copy a cell that has the formatting you want.

2. Select the field where you want to apply the formatting.

3. Click the Paste Formatting button.

4.24. Grouping Dates Based on Source Data Formatting

Problem

In your source data you've formatted the order dates to show as year and month (yyyy-mm). When you add the OrderDate field to the row area of your pivot table, there are several instances of each year-month instead of just one (see the table at the left in Figure 4-7). You want all the orders for each month summarized under one heading.

	Sum of Units			Sum of Units	
3					
4	OrderDate ▼	Total		YrMth ▼	Total
5	2006-01	109		2006-01	588
6	2006-01	138		2006-02	314
7	2006-01	151		2006-03	621
8	2006-01	190		2006-04	415
9	2006-02	56		2006-05	317

Figure 4-7. *Individual dates appear in the OrderDate field in the pivot table at the left; the YrMth field summarizes data in the pivot table at the right.*

Solution

Formatting the source data doesn't change the underlying dates, so they are listed separately in the pivot table row area. Instead of formatting, you can use the pivot table's grouping feature to combine the data by month and year:

1. Right-click the OrderDate field button.

2. Choose Group and Show Detail ➤ Group.

3. In the By list, select Months and Years, then click OK.

Another option is to add another column to the source data, and use a formula to convert the dates to text. Assuming OrderDates are in column A, follow these steps:

1. Add a blank column to the source data table, with the heading YrMth.

2. In the cell below the heading, type the formula **=TEXT(A2,"yyyy-mm")**.

3. Copy this formula down to the last row of data.

4. Refresh the pivot table, then add the YrMth field to the pivot table to replace the OrderDate field (see the table at the right in Figure 4-7).

4.25. Changing Alignment for Merged Labels

Problem

You turned on the Merge labels option in the PivotTable Options dialog box, and all the row item labels are center aligned. When you select a label cell and try to change the alignment, you get an error message.

Solution

Ensure that Enable Selection is turned on, and click at the top of the pivot table column to select all the row field items. Click the Align Left button on the Formatting toolbar to change the alignment for all the items.

■**Note** When the pivot table is refreshed or changed, the merged labels will return to center alignment, and will have to be reformatted.

4.26. Displaying Line Breaks in Pivot Table Cells

Problem

Some fields in your data have line breaks (Alt+Enter). In the pivot table, these appear as a small square instead of a line break.

Solution

In the pivot table, format the cells to show the line break character:

1. In the pivot table, select the items that you want to have line breaks.

2. Choose Format ➤ Cells, and on the Alignment tab, add a checkmark to Wrap text.

3. Click OK.

4.27. Showing Only the Top Items

Problem

You want to show data for the top ten salespeople and hide the others.

Solution

You can use the Top 10 AutoShow feature to hide the salespeople:

1. Double-click the Salesperson field button to open the PivotTable Field dialog box.

2. Click the Advanced button.

3. For Top 10 AutoShow, select On, and set the Show option to Top 10.

Note The Top 10 AutoShow feature may not work as expected in a pivot table based on an OLAP cube. For example, instead of showing the top ten salespeople per region, it would show the sales per region of the top ten salespeople overall.

4.28. Freezing Heading Rows

Problem

Your pivot table is quite large and you want to keep the row and column headings visible as you work.

Solution

You can freeze the cells at the top and left of the window:

1. Select the cell below and to the right of the cells you want to freeze. For example, to freeze rows 1:5, and columns A:C, select cell D6.

2. Choose Window ➤ Freeze Panes.

4.29. Using the Always Display Items Option

Problem

The PivotTable toolbar has an Always Display Items button, but clicking it doesn't have any effect on your pivot table.

Solution

You won't see the effect of this setting unless all the data fields are removed from the pivot table. If the Always Display Items option is turned on, the row and column fields will continue to show items, even if all data fields are removed. If the Always Display Items option is turned off and all data fields are removed, the row and column field items will be hidden.

4.30. Applying Number Formatting to Page Fields

Problem

You want to change the date format of a field in the page area. When you right-click the field button and choose Field Settings, to open the PivotTable Field dialog box, the Number button isn't visible.

Solution

If a numeric field in the data table contains blank cells, or cells with text, then the Number button won't be displayed in the PivotTable Field dialog box for the pivot table field, except in the data area. Fill the blank cells in the source data, and remove any text, and you'll be able to format the pivot table field.

4.31. Displaying Hyperlinks

Problem

There are hyperlinks in your source data, but when you add these fields to the pivot table, the hyperlinks don't appear.

Solution

The pivot table can't show hyperlinks from the source data, and you can't add hyperlinks to the pivot table. You could add a formula outside the pivot table, to create a hyperlink:

```
=IF(LEFT(B13,3)="www",HYPERLINK("http://"&B13),"")
```

but these formulas could be lost if the pivot table changes.

4.32. Changing Total Label Text

Problem

You tried to change the text in the Total label to something more descriptive, but got an error message: "Cannot change this part of a pivot report."

Solution

If your pivot table has only one data field, and either the row or column area has no fields, you'll see the label Total instead of Grand Total. The Total label can't be changed.

4.33. Changing Subtotal Label Text

Problem

You want to change the text in the Subtotal labels to make it more descriptive.

Solution

If you select a cell that contains a subtotal label, and type a new label that doesn't contain the item name, each item subtotal in the field will display that same text in its label. For example, if you change a subtotal label from Plan Total to Budget Subtotal, every item in the field will have Budget Subtotal as its subtotal label.

However, if you include the item name in the revised label, each item subtotal will retain its unique identifier. For example, in a field that shows the sales manager's name, you can change the first subtotal label from Smith Total to Subtotal--Smith. The subtotal for all other sales managers will show the person's name, preceded by Subtotal.

■**Caution** These changes will not be undone if you reset the pivot table captions.

4.34. Formatting Date Field Subtotal Labels

Problem

You formatted a date field as dd-mmm-yy, but its subtotal label is showing the short date format, like the dates in the source data table.

Solution

Change the formatting in the PivotTable Field dialog box instead of selecting cells and changing the format:

1. Right-click the field button or Field heading cell, and choose Field Settings.

2. Click the Number button, and select the date formatting option you want.

3. Click OK to close the Format Cells dialog box, and click OK to close the PivotTable Field dialog box.

4.35. Showing Additional Subtotals

Problem

The outer row field in your pivot table has subtotals that show the sum for each item. You'd like another set of subtotals to show the average for each item.

Solution

You can format the field to show more subtotal rows:

1. Double-click the row field button to open the PivotTable Field dialog box.

2. In the list of Summary functions, click on each function that you want to use as a subtotal, then click OK.

Note Unlike with the regular subtotal headings, you can't change the text in these multiple subtotals.

4.36. Showing Subtotals for Inner Fields

Problem

You want to show subtotals for the innermost row or column fields.

Solution

When added to the pivot table, the innermost fields in the row and column areas don't automatically display subtotals. You can format the fields to show subtotals:

1. Double-click the field button to open the PivotTable Field dialog box.

2. In the list of Summary functions, click on each function that you want to use as a subtotal, then click OK.

All the subtotals for the innermost field will appear after the last item.

4.37. Changing the Grand Total Label Text

Problem

There's one data field in the pivot table, and you would like to change the text in the Grand Total labels.

Solution

You can change all or part of the Row Grand Total text or the Column Grand Total text by typing over the cell or editing in the cell or formula bar.

■**Note** If you change the label for either of these Grand Totals, the other will automatically display the revised text.

4.38. Changing Labels for Grand Totals

Problem

There are multiple data fields in the pivot table, and you would like to change the text in the Grand Total labels.

Solution

You can't change the Row Grand Total text if there are multiple data fields arranged horizontally. You can't change the Column Grand Total text if there are multiple data fields arranged vertically.

4.39. Displaying Grand Totals at Top of Pivot Table

Problem

You'd like the Row Grand Totals to be at the top of the pivot table instead of the bottom.

Solution

You can't change the Grand Total position in the pivot table. If displayed, the Row Grand Total will be at the bottom of the pivot table, and the Column Grand Total will be at the right.

4.40. Hiding Grand Totals

Problem

In your pivot table you have Sum of Units and Units as % of Row. You'd like to hide the Grand Total for % of Row, because every row is 100%.

Solution

You could change the font color to white for the % of Row grand total. The column will appear empty, and the results will stay hidden, even if you pivot the data in the table.

4.41. Using a Worksheet Template

Problem

You created a worksheet template named Sheet.xlt, and stored it in your XLSTART folder. When you create a new pivot table with the PivotTable and PivotChart Wizard, it doesn't use your worksheet template.

Solution

Insert a new worksheet, which will use your worksheet template (Insert ➤ Worksheet). Then, cut the pivot table from the unformatted worksheet, and paste it onto the new sheet. Or, record a macro as you apply the headers, footer, and other settings from your worksheet template. After you create a pivot table, run that macro to apply the settings.

4.42. Displaying Multiple Pivot Tables in a Dashboard

Problem

You want to show multiple pivot tables on one worksheet, as part of an Executive Summary Report (Dashboard).

Solution

Create each pivot table on a separate worksheet, so you don't have problems with overlapping. Then, use the Camera tool to create a linked picture of each pivot table on the Dashboard.

Tip This technique works best if the pivot table layouts are static. If the layout changes and extends beyond the linked range, a new linked picture will be required on the Dashboard.

Adding the Camera Tool to Your Toolbar

1. Choose Tools ➤ Customize.

2. On the Commands tab, select the Tools category.

3. In the list of Commands, select the Camera tool, and drag it to one of your toolbars (see Figure 4-8).

4. Close the Customize dialog box.

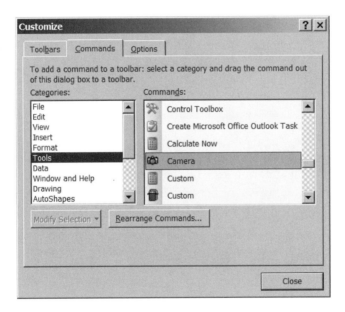

Figure 4-8. *The Camera tool in the Customize dialog box*

Adding a Pivot Table to the Dashboard Using the Camera Tool

1. Select the pivot table cells. You may wish to include a blank row and column beyond the pivot table edges.

2. Click the Camera tool button.

3. On the Dashboard worksheet, click the cell where you'd like the top-left corner of the pivot table, and the Camera tool will paste a linked picture of the pivot table.

■**Note** Because the picture is linked, if the pivot table contents change, the picture will be updated automatically.

---

4. If required, resize and reposition the linked picture, and format the border and fill color.

Adding a Pivot Table to the Dashboard Without Using the Camera Tool

1. Select the pivot table cells. You may wish to include a blank row and column beyond the pivot table edges.

2. Choose Edit ➤ Copy.

3. On the Dashboard worksheet, select the cell where you'd like the top-left corner of the pivot table.

4. Hold the Shift key, and choose Edit ➤ Paste Picture Link.

5. Resize and reposition the linked picture, if required.

■**Tip** Using this method, the picture is created with no border and no default fill color.

CHAPTER 5

■■■

Extracting Pivot Table Data

After you create a pivot table, you may want to extract some of the summarized data for use in other parts of the workbook. The GetPivotData worksheet function can be used for retrieving specific data from the pivot table. Another way to extract data is to use the Drill to Details feature, which returns records from the source data for the selected pivot table cell. Finally, the Show Pages feature can be used to create copies of the pivot table on newly inserted worksheets.

Note The GetPivotData examples shown in this chapter are for Excel 2002 and Excel 2003. The arguments required for earlier versions are different. Refer to Excel's Help for examples.

5.1. Using Drill to Details: Extracting Underlying Data
Problem

Your pivot table summarizes sales results, and shows three units sold in January with no product name. You want to see more detail on those units.

Solution

For pivot tables that are based on non-OLAP source data, you can use the pivot table's Drill to Details feature to extract the source data. For this example, in the pivot table simply double-click the cell that contains the 3.

The Drill to Details feature extracts the records that contribute to the summarized data, and sends the records to a new sheet in the active workbook.

Tip Instead of double-clicking a cell, you can select a cell in the data area of the pivot table, and click the Show Detail button on the PivotTable toolbar.

How It Works

By using the information stored in the pivot table's pivot cache, this technique should create a new sheet with the related records from the original source data. It's a good way to investigate anomalies in the summarized data. If the Drill to Details feature doesn't work, one of the following problems may offer an explanation.

5.2. Using Drill to Details: Re-creating Source Data Table

Problem

Someone accidentally deleted the worksheet that contained the source data for your pivot table, and you would like to re-create it. (Yes, you know that you should have kept a backup copy!)

Solution

You may be able to use the pivot table's Drill to Details feature to re-create the source data:

1. Ensure that none of the items in the visible fields are hidden. Each page field should have (All) selected, and the (Show All) item should be checked in each of the row and column fields.

Tip You don't need to include all fields in the pivot table in order to see them in the Drill to Details output. A pivot table with just one field in the data area, and nothing in the row, column, or page fields, can output all the source data when the grand total cell is double-clicked.

---

2. If the grand totals for rows and grand totals for columns aren't visible, right-click a cell in the PivotTable report and choose Table Options. Check the options Grand totals for rows and Grand totals for columns, then click OK.

3. Double-click the grand total cell at the bottom right of the pivot table.

This should create a new sheet with the related records from the original source data. If the source table contained formulas, you will have to re-create them, as the Drill to Details feature exports the data only. If the Drill to Details feature doesn't work, one of the following recipes may offer an explanation.

How It Works

The Drill to Details feature, where available, will create a new worksheet with the records from the source data that are included in the amount shown in the double-clicked cell. The columns are in the same order as those in the source data, and the list is formatted with Table AutoFormat List 3.

The records exported in the Drill to Details process are from the current pivot cache. If you had made changes to the source data and not yet updated the pivot table, those changes would not be reflected in the exported records.

If you rename the sheet that was created during the Drill to Details process, using the same name as the worksheet that originally held the source data, the pivot cache may automatically connect to the new source data table. If not, you can connect to the new source range:

1. Right-click a cell in the pivot table, and choose PivotTable Wizard.

2. Click the Back button, and select the new source data table range.

3. Click Finish.

Tip If your pivot table is based on a named range, you may have to redefine the named range if the original range was deleted.

5.3. Using Drill to Details: Receiving Error Messages in a Non-OLAP Pivot Table

Problem

The Drill to Details feature isn't working in your pivot table, and it's not OLAP based. An error message says, "Cannot change this part of a PivotTable report."

Solution

The Drill to Details feature may be turned off in the PivotTable Options dialog box. To turn it on, follow these steps:

1. Right-click a cell in the pivot table, and choose Table Options.

2. Add a checkmark to Enable drill to details.

3. Click OK to close the PivotTable Options dialog box.

5.4. Using Drill to Details: Receiving the Saved Without Underlying Data Error Message
Problem

The Drill to Details feature isn't working in your pivot table, and it's not OLAP based. An error message says "The PivotTable report was saved without the underlying data. Use the Refresh Data command to update the report."

Solution

The Save data with table layout option may have been turned off in the PivotTable Options dialog box. To refresh the PivotTable report, click the Refresh button on the PivotTable toolbar. After refreshing the pivot table, you'll be able to use the Drill to Details feature.

How It Works

To reduce the file size, when a pivot table is based on an external data source, the Save data with table layout option can be turned off in the PivotTable Options dialog box. The cached data isn't saved when the workbook is closed, so this creates a smaller Excel file that may open, close, and save faster.

However, you have to refresh the pivot table to update the pivot cache before you can use it. The refresh creates a copy of the cached data that the Drill to Details feature can use to export the underlying records to a new worksheet.

For convenience, if the Save data with table layout option can be turned off, you can set the PivotTable report to refresh automatically when the file opens:

1. Right-click a cell in the pivot table, and choose Table Options.

2. Add a checkmark to Refresh on open.

3. Click OK to close the PivotTable Options dialog box.

5.5. Using Drill to Details: Formatting
Problem

When you use the Drill to Details feature, data is exported to a new worksheet. You want the data in this sheet to use the same formatting as the source data.

Solution

There's no way to control the format of the data that's exported during a Drill to Details operation. After it's been exported, you can format the results.

To manually format the data, use the Format Painter button on the Excel Formatting toolbar to copy the formatting from the source data and apply it to the detail sheet.

5.6. Using Drill to Details: New Sheets Are Not Using the Worksheet Template
Problem

You created a worksheet template named Sheet.xlt, and stored it in your XLSTART folder. When you use the Drill to Details feature, it creates a new sheet with the details but doesn't use your worksheet template.

Solution

Insert a new worksheet, which will use your worksheet template (Insert ➤ Worksheet). Then, cut the detail from the unformatted worksheet and paste it onto the new sheet. Or, record a macro as you apply the headers, footer, and other settings from your worksheet template. After you use the Drill to Details feature, run that macro to apply the settings on the new worksheet. For information on recording macros, see Chapter 13.

5.7. Using Drill to Details: Updating Source Data
Problem

After you use the Drill to Details feature, you change some of the data in the output sheet. The changes aren't reflected in the source data.

Solution

The Drill to Details output isn't connected to the source data, and changes made there won't affect the source data. Make the changes in the source data directly. Then, you could use the Drill to Details feature again to output the revised data.

Also, changes to the source data won't be displayed in previous Drill to Details output sheets. If the source data changes, you may need to create new Drill to Details output.

5.8. Using Drill to Details: Outputting Specific Fields
Problem

When you use the Drill to Details feature, you don't want all the fields to appear in the output sheet, but just the fields that are visible in the pivot table.

Solution

If Drill to Details is used in a pivot table, all columns from the source data will be shown. If all columns in the source data aren't required in the pivot table, rearrange the source data, moving those columns you don't want included to the far left or right of the source table. Then, base the pivot table on columns that can be shown in the Drill to Details output.

5.9. Using Drill to Details: Preventing Sheet Creation
Problem

When you use the Drill to Details feature, data is exported to a new worksheet. You'd prefer to place the details on an existing worksheet to prevent new sheets from being created.

Solution

There's no way to prevent the new sheet from being created. You can copy the details to another sheet after the detail list has been created. If you need this feature frequently, you can create a macro to move the list programmatically. See Chapter 13 for programming information.

5.10. Using Drill to Details: Deleting Created Sheets
Problem

When you use the Drill to Details feature, data is exported to a new worksheet. This creates extra work for you, as you have to delete all the created sheets before closing the workbook.

Solution

Save the workbook just before you use the Drill to Details feature. Then, close the workbook without saving the changes, after viewing the additional sheets that are created by the Drill to Details feature. Or, save the workbook with a new name to preserve the original workbook without the extra worksheets.

5.11. Using GetPivotData: Automatically Inserting a Formula
Problem

You want to refer to a pivot table cell in one of your worksheet formulas so you can perform calculations using the summarized data. When you type an equal sign, then click a cell in the pivot table, Excel inserts a GetPivotData formula:

```
=GETPIVOTDATA("AmtPaid",$A$7,"Partner","Baker")
```

When you try to copy the formula down the worksheet, the results are the same in every row. You would prefer a simple cell reference, like =B5.

Solution

Instead of typing an equal sign, then clicking a cell in the pivot table, you can type the cell reference yourself. For example, type **=B5** instead of clicking cell B5 to create the reference.

How It Works

The GetPivotData worksheet function extracts data from the pivot table for a specific pivot field and pivot item. By default, a GetPivotData formula is automatically created when you refer to a pivot table cell in a worksheet formula. You can turn this feature on or off.

Although the GetPivotData formula looks complex, and you're more comfortable using a simple cell reference, you may get more reliable results by using the GetPivotData function, especially if you plan to add items to the pivot table source.

If you refer to a cell in the pivot table by using a cell reference, the result will be whatever is currently in that cell. Today it might be Total Sales for the West Region, but tomorrow it may be Total Sales for Pencils in the East Region. If you use a GetPivotData formula, the result will check the pivot field items and data and return the result from the correct location in the table, as long as the referenced items and data are still in the pivot table. If the referenced items and data aren't visible in the pivot table, you'll see an error instead of incorrect data.

Tip To ensure that the referenced fields and items remain visible, you could create a pivot table based on the main pivot table and stored on a hidden sheet. In your GetPivotData formulas, refer to this hidden pivot table. Users can change the layout of the main pivot table, and it won't affect your GetPivotData formula results.

The GetPivotData function requires two arguments:

=GETPIVOTDATA(data_field,pivot_table)

For example, the formula

=GETPIVOTDATA("AmtPaid",$A$7)

would return the total Amount Paid in the pivot table located at cell A7.

■Tip For non-OLAP based pivot tables, the data_field argument can be the displayed name, for example, Sum of AmtPaid, or the field name, AmtPaid.

Also, you can include up to 14 pairs of pivot fields and pivot items in the GetPivotData function, after the pivot_table argument:

=GETPIVOTDATA("AmtPaid",$A$7,field1,item1,...)

■Tip The field/item pairs can be in any order, following the data_field and pivot_table arguments, but the related field and item must be listed together, with the field name followed by the item name.

Using the optional field/item pairs allows you to extract specific details from the pivot table. For example, adding one field/item pair, as shown here

=GETPIVOTDATA("AmtPaid",$A$7,"Partner","Baker")

would return the total Amount Paid for the partner named Baker, in the pivot table located at cell A7. Partner is a pivot field, and Baker is an item in the Partner field.

Expanding the previous formula with two field/item pairs, as shown here

=GETPIVOTDATA("AmtPaid",$A$7,"Partner","Baker","Service","Tax")

would return the total Amount Paid for the partner named Baker for Tax services in the pivot table located at cell A7. Service is a pivot field, and Tax is an item in the Service field.

■Note Since a GetPivotData formula can only display visible data from the pivot table, it's best suited to a pivot table that has the referenced fields in the row or column areas, and limited pivoting of the fields used in the GetPivotData formula.

5.12. Using GetPivotData: Turning Off Automatic Insertion of Formulas
Problem

Excel inserts a GetPivotData formula every time you try to link to a cell in the pivot table. You want to turn off this feature.

Solution

You can add the Generate GetPivotData button to your PivotTable toolbar to toggle this feature on and off:

1. At the end of the PivotTable toolbar, click the Toolbar Options arrow.

Note If the PivotTable toolbar is floating, the Toolbar Options arrow is to the left of the Close button, at the top right of the toolbar. To dock the toolbar, double-click its title bar.

---

2. Select Add or Remove Buttons ➤ PivotTable.

3. Select Generate GetPivotData to add the button to the PivotTable toolbar (see Figure 5-1).

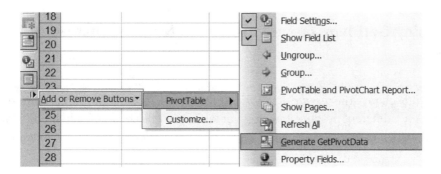

Figure 5-1. *Add the Generate GetPivotData button to the PivotTable toolbar.*

On the PivotTable toolbar, click the Generate GetPivotData button to toggle this feature on and off.

If you'd prefer to have the Generate GetPivotData button on a different toolbar, you can add it by using the Customize dialog box:

1. Choose Tools ➤ Customize, and select the Commands tab.

2. In the Categories list, select the Data category.

3. Near the end of the list of commands, select the Generate GetPivotData button, and drag it to one of your toolbars.

4. Close the Customize dialog box.

5.13. Using GetPivotData: Referencing Pivot Tables in Other Workbooks
Problem

Your GetPivotData formula refers to a pivot table in another workbook. When you open the workbook and update the links, you get a #REF! error in the GetPivotData formulas.

Solution

The GetPivotData function, like some other Excel functions, only returns data for references in the same file, or another open file. To see the results of the GetPivotData formula, open the workbook that contains the referenced pivot table.

Or, create the GetPivotData formula in the workbook that contains the pivot table, perhaps on a hidden worksheet. Then, in the second workbook, link to the cell that contains the GetPivotData formula in the first workbook.

5.14. Using GetPivotData: Using Cell References Instead of Text Strings
Problem

You frequently change the text strings in the GetPivotData formula when you want to see the results for a different product in your pivot table. It's time consuming to modify the formula, and it's easy to make a mistake as you edit the product names in the formula.

Solution

You can replace the text strings in the GetPivotData formula with references to cells that contain the text you want to extract. For example, instead of a formula that contains a Partner name, like this one:

```
=GETPIVOTDATA("AmtPaid",$A$7,"Partner","Baker")
```

type the name in cell B5, then change the formula to

`=GETPIVOTDATA("AmtPaid",$A$7,"Partner",B5)`

■**Tip** Use the Generate GetPivotData feature to create the formula by clicking a cell in the pivot table. Then, in the formula, highlight a text string and its enclosing quotation marks, and click the cell you want to use as a reference for this text.

Type a different Partner name in the referenced cell, and the formula will show the results for the new name. It's much quicker and easier than adjusting a small part of the formula.

■**Note** The referenced cell should contain only the text, not the double quotes that surround the text in the formula.

How It Works

Using a cell reference instead of a text string makes the formula more flexible. For example, on an executive summary sheet, you can create a GetPivotData formula that refers to a cell that contains a product name. Then, change the product name to see a different result from the pivot table.

To make this easier for users, use the Data Validation feature to create a dropdown list of valid selections in the referenced cell. In this example, the cell should contain a product list, with all the products that are summarized in the pivot table.

To create a dropdown list that updates immediately if there are different products in the pivot table, follow these steps:

1. On a separate worksheet, named Lists in this example, create a pivot table that's based on the first pivot table.

2. In the row area, add the Product field, and in the data area, add the Qty field.

3. Set the Product field to Ascending sort.

4. In the pivot table, turn off Grand totals for columns.

5. To create a dynamic named range for the product list, choose Insert ➤ Name ➤ Define.

6. Type a one-word name for the list, for example, **ProductList**.

7. In the Refers to box, type an OFFSET formula that counts the cells with data, and subtracts the heading cells with text, for example

```
=OFFSET(Lists!$A$5,0,0,COUNTA(Lists!$A:$A)-
    COUNTA(Lists!$A$1:$A$4),1)
```

as shown in Figure 5-2.

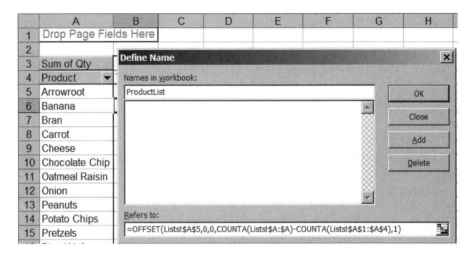

Figure 5-2. *Create a dynamic named range.*

8. Click OK to close the Define Name dialog box.

9. On the Summary sheet, select the cell where you want the dropdown list.

10. Choose Data ➤ Validation.

11. From the Allow dropdown, choose List.

12. In the Source box, type an equal sign, and the name of the dynamic range:

```
=ProductList
```

13. Click OK to close the Data Validation dialog box.

14. Select an item from the data validation dropdown list, and the results of the GetPivotData formula that refer to the cell will change.

▬Tip Because the second pivot table is based on the first pivot table, it will automatically be refreshed when you update the first pivot table. This will ensure that all the products appear in the data validation list.

5.15. Using GetPivotData: Using Cell References in an OLAP-Based Pivot Table
Problem

You want to replace some of the text strings in the GetPivotData formulas that refer to your OLAP-based pivot table. You're having trouble getting the syntax right, and the formulas are returning #REF! errors.

Solution

Because the OLAP data is in levels, those levels are included in the GetPivotData arguments. When you link to a cell in an OLAP-based pivot table, the resulting formula may look similar to this:

```
=GETPIVOTDATA("[Measures].[Sum Of Qty]",$A$4,
    "[Region]","[Region].[All].[West]"))
```

If you'd like to refer to a Region name in cell H3, you can replace that part of the formula with a cell reference:

```
=GETPIVOTDATA("[Measures].[Sum Of Qty]",$A$4,
    "[Region]","[Region].[All].[" & H3 & "]"))
```

■**Note** The square brackets in the field and item names mark the start and end of the level names. When replacing text with a cell reference, do not delete the square brackets from the formula, or the formula will return an error.

5.16. Using GetPivotData: Preventing Cell Reference Errors for Data_Field
Problem

When you use a cell reference as the data_field argument in a GetPivotData formula, the result is an error. For example, this formula works:

```
=GETPIVOTDATA("AmtPaid",$A$7,"Partner","Baker")
```

but this returns a #REF! error:

```
=GETPIVOTDATA(E3,$A$7,"Partner","Baker")
```

although cell E3 contains the text "AmtPaid".

Solution

To use a cell reference in the data_field argument, concatenate an empty string at the start or end of the reference. For example, you could use

```
=GETPIVOTDATA("" & E3,$A$7,"Partner","Baker")
```

or

```
=GETPIVOTDATA(E3 & "",$A$7,"Partner","Baker")
```

5.17. Using GetPivotData: Preventing Errors in Data_Fields for OLAP-Based Pivot Tables
Problem

In a GetPivotData formula that refers to your OLAP-based pivot table, you used [Measures].[Qty] as the data_field argument, and the formula is returning a #REF! error. Qty is the name of the measures field in your database.

Solution

In the GetPivotData formula for a non-OLAP-based pivot table, you can use the field name (Qty), or the displayed field name (Sum of Qty). However, in the GetPivotData formula for an OLAP-based pivot table, there's no difference between the names, and you should use the name as displayed in the Pivot Field list, for example, Sum of Qty:

```
=GETPIVOTDATA("[Measures].[Sum Of Qty]",$A$4,
    "[Region]","[Region].[All].[West]")
```

5.18. Using GetPivotData: Extracting Data for Blank Field Items
Problem

A row field item is shown as (blank) in your pivot table, and you want to extract the total for this item using a GetPivotData formula.

Solution

In the formula, leave an empty reference where the item name argument would appear. For example, the formula to return the total for ABC Ltd is

```
=GETPIVOTDATA("Amount",$A$7,"Customer","ABC Ltd")
```

and for the (blank) customer item

```
=GETPIVOTDATA("Amount",$A$7,"Customer",)
```

If you're using cell references in the formula, the referenced cell should contain the text (blank). For example, if cell G2 contains (blank), the following formula will return the total Amount for the (blank) customer item:

```
=GETPIVOTDATA("Amount",$A$7,"Customer",G2)
```

5.19. Using GetPivotData: Preventing Errors for Missing Field Items
Problem

You use a GetPivotData formula to return the total for each product per salesperson per month. Some months, a salesperson may have zero sales for a product, so there's no value in the pivot table. This results in #REF! errors being returned by the GetPivotData formulas, which in turn affects other formulas, such as SUM.

Solution

You can use the ISERROR function to prevent the error from being returned. For example:

```
=IF(ISERROR(GETPIVOTDATA("Units",$A$3,"Item","Pencils")),"",
  GETPIVOTDATA("Units",$A$3,"Item","Pencils"))
```

This returns an empty string if the result of the GetPivotData is an error. Or, you could alter the formula slightly to return a zero instead:

```
=IF(ISERROR(GETPIVOTDATA("Units",$A$3,"Item","Pencils")),0,
  GETPIVOTDATA("Units",$A$3,"Item","Pencils"))
```

5.20. Using GetPivotData: Referencing Two Pivot Tables
Problem

To make your data easier to read, you have the data displayed in two small pivot tables. You'd like to show the combined total in a summary report on another worksheet.

Solution

Use two GetPivotData functions in one formula. For example, use this to calculate the total number of new policies in two pivot tables on the InsurPivot worksheet:

```
=GETPIVOTDATA("Policies",InsurPivot!$A$5,"Status","New") +
   GETPIVOTDATA("Policies",InsurPivot!$J$5,"Status","New")
```

■Tip If Status is in the column area, the Column Grand Totals must be visible, or the formula will return a #REF! error.

5.21. Using GetPivotData: Preventing Errors for Custom Subtotals
Problem

Instead of showing a Sum for your row field items, you used Average as a custom Subtotal. You created a link to one of the subtotal cells, and a GetPivotData formula was automatically created. It looks different than the other GetPivotData formulas on the worksheet, and returns a #REF! error:

```
=GETPIVOTDATA($A$5,"InsType[Auto;Data,Average] New")
```

If you use the Automatic subtotal, the GetPivotData formula that's created is

```
=GETPIVOTDATA("Policies",$A$5,"InsType","Auto","Status","New")
```

and it returns a correct result.

Solution

When custom subtotals are used, the automatically generated GetPivotData formulas that refer to those subtotals return a #REF! error. Even if you select SUM as the custom function, the result is an error, although using the Automatic function, which shows a SUM, will return a correct result.

To fix the formula so it calculates correctly, remove the "Data," from the formula. The corrected formula for the previous example is

```
=GETPIVOTDATA($A$5,"InsType[Auto;Average] New")
```

5.22. Using GetPivotData: Preventing Errors for Date References
Problem

Your GetPivotData formula contains a date, and although that date is visible in the pivot table, the formula is returning an error:

```
=GETPIVOTDATA("AmtPaid",$A$7,"DateBilled","1/5/06")
```

Solution

If the date is in the pivot table but formatted differently, the GetPivotData formula will produce a #REF! error. Instead of entering the date as a text string, you can use the DATE function. For example:

```
=GETPIVOTDATA("AmtPaid",$A$7,"DateBilled",DATE(2006,1,5))
```

The arguments of the DATE function are Year, Month, and Day.
     Or, you can enter a valid date in a worksheet cell, then refer to that cell in the GetPivotData formula:

```
=GETPIVOTDATA("AmtPaid",$A$7,"DateBilled",H3)
```

where cell H3 contains a valid date.

5.23. Using GetPivotData: Referring to a Pivot Table
Problem

When you create a GetPivotData formula, it includes a reference to a cell in the pivot table as the second argument. In this example, your pivot table is located at cell A7:

```
=GETPIVOTDATA("AmtPaid",$A$7)
```

You'd like to type a cell address on the worksheet, and have the GetPivotData use a pivot table located at that cell. For example, you want to type **H6** in cell E1, and see the total amount paid in that pivot table.

Solution

You can use the INDIRECT function in the GetPivotData function to create a range reference based on the text in cell E1. For example:

```
=GETPIVOTDATA("AmtPaid",INDIRECT(E1))
```

If you type **A7** in cell E1, the formula will return the total from the first pivot table, and if you type **H6** in cell E1, the formula will return the total from the second pivot table.

How It Works

The INDIRECT function requires one argument:

```
=INDIRECT(ref_text)
```

and returns the range specified by the reference text argument. You can type the reference text directly in the formula:

```
=INDIRECT("A7")
```

or refer to a cell that contains the reference text:

```
=INDIRECT(E1)
```

where cell E1 contains the text A7.

5.24. Using Show Pages: Creating Pivot Table Copies
Problem

You'd like to create a separate copy of the pivot table for each sales manager to make it easier for them to focus on their customers' sales results.

Solution

The Show Pages feature creates a copy of the pivot table on a separate worksheet for each item in the selected page field. It's a quick way to create multiple versions of the pivot table for viewing or printing.

Follow these steps to create the copies:

1. Move the Sales Manager field to the pivot table page area.

2. Select a cell in the pivot table.

3. On the PivotTable toolbar, choose PivotTable ➤ Show Pages.

4. In the Show Pages window, select the page field for which you want to create the pages, then click OK.

■Tip If a page field is the active cell on the worksheet, when the Show Pages window opens, that field will be selected in the list of page fields. Otherwise, the first page field on the worksheet will be selected in the list.

How It Works

A copy of the pivot table, on a new worksheet, is created for each item in the field you select in the Show Pages window. The new sheet is named the same as the field item, and that item is selected in the page field.

■**Note** A copy of the pivot table is not created for the (All) item, or the (Multiple Items) selection.

Most formatting from the original pivot table should be retained, except formatting that would normally be lost when the pivot table is changed. Conditional formatting will be lost.

Each copy is based on the original pivot table, and uses the same pivot cache, so this technique should have a minimal impact on the file size.

Only the pivot table is copied; other data on the same sheet as the original pivot table is not copied, nor are page settings, such as footers and margins. If you want to include other data, such as formulas in cells adjacent to the pivot table, you can use the Edit ➤ Move or Copy Sheet command to create a copy of the worksheet, instead of using the Show Pages command.

5.25. Using Show Pages: Creating Incorrect Sheet Names
Problem

You used the Show Pages feature to create a copy of your pivot table for each customer. Most sheets had the customer name on the sheet tab, but one was named Sheet5, and one name was shortened.

Solution

When the sheets are created, normal sheet name rules are followed.

- The following characters can't be used in a sheet name:

  : \ / ? * [ ]

  If the customer name contains one of those characters, a generic name, for example, Sheet5, will be used for that customer's sheet.

- The maximum number of characters allowed in a sheet name is 31. Only the first 26 characters of the customer name will be used.

- If a sheet already exists with the customer name, or the first 26 characters of the customer's name, a new sheet will be created with "(2)" appended to the name.

5.26. Using Show Pages: Not Creating Sheets for All Items
Problem

You used the Show Pages feature to create a copy of your pivot table for each customer. However, sheets weren't created for all customers.

Solution

Some of the customers may be hidden in the page field. To show them, follow these steps:

1. Double-click the Customer field button.

2. In the Hide items list, any item that's highlighted has been hidden (see Figure 5-3).

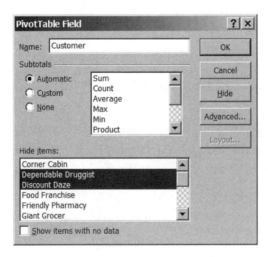

Figure 5-3. *Click on a highlighted item to remove the highlighting.*

3. Click on a highlighted item to remove the highlighting.

4. Click OK to close the PivotTable Field dialog box.

5.27. Using Show Pages: Not Formatting New Sheets
Problem

You created a worksheet template named Sheet.xlt, and stored it in your XLSTART folder. When you use the Show Pages feature, it creates a new sheet for each page item but doesn't use your worksheet template.

Solution

You can copy the formatting from the original pivot table worksheet:

1. Select the original pivot table worksheet.

2. Hold down the Ctrl key, and select the sheets created by the Show Pages command.

3. With the original pivot table sheet as the active sheet, choose File ➤ Page Setup.

4. Without changing any settings, click OK to close the Page Setup dialog box.

5. To ungroup the sheets, right-click one of the selected sheet tabs, and choose Ungroup Sheets.

Or, record a macro as you apply the headers, footer, and other settings from your worksheet template. After you use the Drill to Details feature, run the recorded macro to apply the settings on the new worksheet. See Chapter 13 for programming information.

5.28. Using Show Pages: Enabling the Show Pages Command
Problem

You want to create a copy of the pivot table for each customer, and the Customer field is in the page area. However, the Show Pages command is disabled on the PivotTable menu, and you can't create the copies.

Solution

If the pivot table is based on an external source, the Customer page field may be set to query the external data when a different page is selected. This PivotTable option reduces the memory required but prevents the Show Pages feature from being used. Follow these steps to change the setting:

1. In the pivot table, right-click the Customer Page field, and choose Field Settings.

2. Click the Advanced button.

3. Under Page field options, select Retrieve external data for all page fields (faster performance).

4. Click OK to close the PivotTable Field Advanced Options dialog box.

5. Click OK to close the PivotTable Field dialog box.

CHAPTER 6

Modifying a Pivot Table

After you create a pivot table, you can modify it. You can move the fields to a different part of the pivot table, add or remove fields, show or hide items, and make other changes. For some of these tasks, you can use the PivotTable toolbar, which you can also modify, to make your work easier.

6.1. Using Page Fields: Shifting Up When Adding Page Fields
Problem

In the rows above your pivot table, you've entered some worksheet heading text. You dragged another field to the page area, below the existing page field (see Figure 6-1). When you release the mouse button, you get a warning: "Do you want to replace the contents of the destination cells in PivotSheet?" If you click OK, the page fields move up and remove the heading. You'd prefer that the page fields move down so they don't delete the worksheet heading that you've entered in the first few rows.

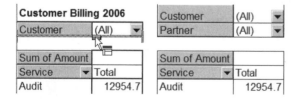

Figure 6-1. *Adding a page field deletes text in cells above the pivot table.*

Solution

When you add fields to the page area, Excel tries to keep the main section of the pivot table in its current position. Existing page fields are pushed up to prevent the main section from moving down. There isn't a setting you can change to prevent this, but one of the following workarounds may help:

- Instead of arranging the page fields vertically, change them to a horizontal layout, as described in the following section.

- If you have headings on the worksheet, above the pivot table, leave a few blank rows between them and the pivot table. If necessary, add extra rows before adding fields to the page area.

- If the heading information is only required for printing, you could move the heading text to the Header (View ➤ Header and Footer), where it won't be affected by changes to the pivot table layout.

6.2. Using Page Fields: Arranging Fields Horizontally
Problem

You have many fields in the page area, and they're pushing the pivot table down on the worksheet. You'd like to arrange the page fields horizontally, but when you drag them to the right, they're removed from the pivot table.

Solution

You can arrange the page fields horizontally by changing the pivot table options:

1. Right-click a cell in the pivot table, and choose Table Options.

2. From the Page layout dropdown, select an option for arranging the page fields.

3. If you selected Down, then Across, the following dropdown list is labeled "Fields per column." Select the number of page fields you want in each stack.

Note If the Fields per column option is set at zero, the page fields are arranged in a single column.

4. If you selected Across, then Down, the following dropdown list is labeled "Fields per row." Select the number of page fields you want in each row.

Note If the Fields per row option is set at zero, the page fields are arranged in a single row.

5. Click OK to close the PivotTable Options dialog box.

6.3. Using Page Fields: Hiding Entries in Page Field Item List
Problem

The Products field is in the page area of your pivot table. You want to hide some of the products instead of viewing the data for all the items. Unlike the row and column fields, the page field's dropdown list doesn't have check boxes to indicate which items to show and which to hide.

Solution

1. Double-click the page field button to open the PivotTable Field dialog box.

2. In the Hide items list, select the items that you want to hide.

■Tip You can use the navigation keys (Home, End, Page Up, Page Down, arrow keys) to move up and down in the Hide items list, and press the spacebar to select or deselect the items.

---

3. Click the OK button to close the PivotTable Field dialog box.

4. The page field will show (Multiple Items) instead of (All), unless an individual item is selected.

■Tip You could temporarily move the page field to the row area, remove checkmarks for the items you want to hide, and move the field back to the page area.

6.4. Using Page Fields: Hiding Page Field Items in OLAP-Based Pivot Tables
Problem

You want to hide some of the page field items in your OLAP-based pivot table instead of viewing the data for all the items. Unlike the row and column fields, the page field's drop-down list doesn't have check boxes to indicate which fields to show and which to hide. When you double-click the page field button to open the PivotTable Field dialog box, there's no Hide items list.

Solution

1. On the worksheet, click the page field's dropdown arrow to open the list.

2. At the bottom left of the list, add a checkmark to Select multiple items.

3. Use the + sign to expand the list, then add or remove checkmarks to indicate which page field items to show.

4. Check or uncheck an item to affect all the items in the hierarchy below that item.

5. Click the OK button to close the dropdown list.

6. The page field will show (Multiple Items) instead of (All), unless an individual item is selected.

6.5. Using Page Fields: Including Hidden Items in Total
Problem

You hid some of the customers in the Customer page field, but the Total Sales shown in the pivot table didn't change.

Solution

1. Right-click a cell in the pivot table, and choose Table Options.

2. Remove the checkmark from Subtotal hidden page items.

3. Click OK to close the PivotTable Options dialog box.

■**Note** This option is not available for OLAP-based pivot tables.

How It Works

Normally, hidden page items are not included in the pivot table subtotals or grand totals. When you turn on the Subtotal hidden page items option, the items are included.

Also, when page items are hidden, and you select the (All) item from the dropdown list, the cell displays (Multiple Items). If Subtotal hidden page items is on, the cell displays (All).

6.6. Using Page Fields: Filtering for a Date Range
Problem

You'd like to show the total sales for the first 10 days of October, but you don't want to manually hide all the other dates in the Sale Date page field.

Solution

1. Move the Sale Date field to the row area.

2. Right-click the Sale Date field button, and choose Group and Show Detail ➤ Group.

3. In the Grouping dialog box, enter Starting at and Ending at dates.

4. In the By list, select Days, and deselect any other options.

■**Note** If you leave Number of Days set at 1, every day of the year will appear in the field's dropdown list. If you select any other number, only dates in the selected range will appear in the list.

---

5. Click OK to close the Grouping dialog box.

6. In the Sale Date field's dropdown list, uncheck the <10/1/06 and >10/10/06 options that were created.

7. Move the Sale Date field back to the Page area.

6.7. Using Page Fields: Filtering for Future Dates
Problem

You'd like to show the total orders with future ship dates, but you don't want to manually hide all the past dates in the Ship Date page field.

Solution

For some filtering problems, the best solution is to add a column to the source data. In this case, a column can be added to test if the ship date is later than the current date.

1. In the source data table, add a column with the heading ShipLater.

2. In the first data row of the new column, enter a formula that refers to the ShipDate in that row—for example, **=A2 > TODAY()**.

3. Copy the formula down to the last row of data.

4. Refresh the pivot table, and add the ShipLater field to the page area.

5. From the ShipLater page field dropdown list, select TRUE.

■Note Refresh the pivot table each day to see the current calculations for the ShipLater field.

6.8. Using Data Fields: Changing Content in the Data Area
Problem

You'd like to change some of the content in the data area of the pivot table, but when you try, you see the error message "Cannot change this part of a PivotTable report."

Solution

For calculated items, you can select a cell and clear the data, type any number, or change the formula in the formula bar.

■Note If you clear the data in a calculated item cell, you won't be able to make any further changes to that cell.

For other types of data, unless the PivotTable settings are changed programmatically, you can't make any changes to the PivotTable data.

6.9. Using Data Fields: Renaming Fields
Problem

When you add the Units field to the pivot table data area, it's automatically named Sum of Units. You'd like to rename it as Units, but you get an error message: "PivotTable field name already exists."

Solution

To rename a data field on the worksheet, select its field button, or field heading cell, and type a new name. If you try to use the same name as the source data field, you'll see the error message "PivotTable field name already exists."

■**Tip** To avoid this problem, add a space character to the end of the name, and it will be accepted.

To rename a field in the PivotTable and PivotChart Wizard, double-click the field button and type a new name in the Name box. Most names will be accepted, including a single space character or question mark. However, you can't use a field name from the data source, or a name that already exists in the pivot table.

■**Tip** To make the pivot table easier to read, short, descriptive names are best. For example, if a field is named Q3_Sales instead of Third Quarter Sales Total, the column in which it's located can be made much narrower, and it will remain legible. Narrower columns will make the pivot table viewable with less scrolling, and easier to print on one sheet width.

6.10. Using Data Fields: Changing the "Total" Field Name
Problem

When your pivot table contains multiple data fields, the data field names are displayed at the top of the data columns. When there are no column fields and only one data field, the data field name appears at the top left of the pivot table body, and the word Total appears at the top of the data column (see Figure 6-2).

Customer	(All) ▼

Amount	
Service ▼	Total
Audit	12,955
Finance	29,465
Risk	30,845
Tax	34,115
Grand Total	107,380

	Data ▼	
Service ▼	Amount	AmtPaid
Audit	12,955	
Finance	29,465	19,895
Risk	30,845	30,845
Tax	34,115	25,874
Grand Total	107,380	76,614

Figure 6-2. *The pivot table with one data field has Total at the top of its data column. The pivot table with multiple data fields has field names at the top of its data columns.*

Solution

You can't change this behavior, and the text of the Total heading label can't be changed. You could format the label with white font color so that it doesn't appear.

6.11. Using Data Fields: Arranging Horizontally
Problem

You added a second field to the data area, and now the data fields are listed vertically with the row fields. You want them arranged horizontally, with the data field names across the top of the pivot table as column headings.

Solution

To arrange the fields horizontally, drag the Data field button onto the cell that contains the word Total (see Figure 6-3.). Or, if you don't see a cell that contains the word Total, drag the Data field button into the column area of the pivot table.

Service ▼	Data ▼	Total 🔲
Audit	Sum of Amount	12954.7🔲
	Sum of O/S	12954.7
Finance	Sum of Amount	29464.6
	Sum of O/S	9570

Figure 6-3. *Arrange data fields horizontally.*

6.12. Using Data Fields: Restoring Hidden Fields in the Data Field List
Problem

You hid a field that was in the data area, and now you'd like to show it again, but it's missing from the Data field dropdown list.

Solution

When data fields are hidden, they're removed from the pivot table layout. You can drag the field back to the data area from the field list.

How It Works

When you remove a checkmark from the dropdown list in a row field or column field, you're hiding an item in that field. Later, you can show the item again by adding a checkmark to the item.

When you remove a checkmark from the dropdown list in the Data button, you're hiding a data field, not an item. When any field is hidden, it's removed from the pivot table layout. To show the hidden field again, you can drag it back to the pivot table from the field list.

6.13. Using Data Fields: Fixing Source Data Number Fields
Problem

Your source data contains several columns of numbers, such as Quantity, Total Sale, and Deposit Amount. These numbers get summed as zero in the data fields instead of showing the correct totals.

Solution

If you copied the data from another program, such as Microsoft Access, Excel may be seeing the data as text. There are several techniques that you can use to convert the text to numbers in the source data so that they can be summed correctly in the pivot table.

Converting with Paste Special

1. Select a blank cell, and on the Excel Standard toolbar, click the Copy button.

2. Select the cells in the source data that contain the numbers.

3. On the Excel Worksheet menu bar, choose Edit ➤ Paste Special.

4. Click Add, then click OK.

Converting with Text to Columns

1. Select the cells in one column of the source data that contain the numbers.

2. On the Excel Worksheet menu bar, choose Data ➤ Text to Columns.

3. In Step 1 of the Convert Text to Columns Wizard, click Finish.

Converting Dates with Replace All

If dates are formatted with slashes, such as 5/5/06, you can convert them to real dates by replacing the slashes:

1. Select the cells in the source data that contain the dates.

2. On the Excel Worksheet menu bar, choose Edit ➤ Replace.

3. For Find what, type a forward slash: **/**.

4. For Replace with, type a forward slash: **/**.

5. Click Replace All, then click OK to confirm the replacements.

6. Click Close to close the Find and Replace dialog box.

6.14. Using Data Fields: Showing the Source Text Instead of the Count
Problem

When you add the Salesperson field to the data area, it appears as Count of Salesperson instead of showing the salesperson names from the source data.

Solution

You can't display text fields as text in the data area. You could add the Salesperson field to the row area, where the names will be displayed, then use another field in the data area to show a count of the occurrences.

Notes

A limited amount of text can be displayed in the data area by using custom number formats, or the pivot table's options. For example, you can use a custom number format to display the word "Low" in data cells where the SUM is less than 50:

1. Select the data cells in the pivot table.

2. On the Excel Worksheet menu bar, choose Format ➤ Cells.

3. On the Number tab, select the Custom category.

4. In the text box, type **[<50]"Low";General;General**.

5. Click OK.

In another example, you could set the pivot table's options to show N/A instead of empty cells:

1. Right-click a cell in the pivot table, and choose Table Options.

2. Add a checkmark to the For empty cells, show option.

3. In the text box, type **N/A**.

5. Click OK to close the PivotTable Options dialog box.

6.15. Using Pivot Fields: Adding Comments to Pivot Table Cells
Problem

You'd like to add comments to some of the pivot table field headings, or to the data area cells, so that users understand what the fields mean.

Solution

You can add comments to the pivot table, but the comments are attached to the cell, rather than the pivot field. If you change the pivot table layout, the comments won't move with the field, and may create confusion for users instead of helping them.

Instead of comments, you could add an instruction sheet to the workbook, and make your user notes there.

Notes

If you have a calculated item in the pivot table, you can use it to store short notes that are visible in the formula. For example, if a calculated item contains the formula

```
=Shipped + Backordered
```

you can use the N function to add a comment:

```
=Shipped + Backordered + N("This item was discontinued")
```

The note will be visible in the formula bar when the cell is selected.

6.16. Using Pivot Fields: Showing Detail for Inner Fields
Problem

When you select a cell in the outer row field and click the Show Detail button, you see the inner row field items for the selected outer row field. The other row field items aren't affected. However, when you select a cell in an inner row field and click the Show Detail button, it affects all the occurrences of that item. You want to limit the changes to the selected cell.

Solution

Show Detail and Hide Detail affect all occurrences of the item for inner and outer fields. Because there's only one instance of each item in the outer field, it seems to behave differently, but it doesn't. You can't change this feature to hide detail for the selected item only.

How It Works

Show Detail and Hide Detail affect all occurrences of the selected item. For example, in Figure 6-4, the table at the left has all details showing for the fields in the row area. Subtotals for the Category and YearNo fields are set to None.

1. Select the Bars item in the Category field, and click the Hide Detail button on the PivotTable toolbar. Details for the Bars item are hidden.

2. Select the 2005 item in the YearNo field, and click the Hide Detail button on the PivotTable toolbar. Details for the 2005 item are hidden.

Although the 2005 item in the Cookies item was selected when the command was used, 2005 items in both the Cookies and Crackers items are hidden (see the table at the right in Figure 6-4).

Customer (All) ▼

Sum of Qty			
Category ▼	YearNo ▼	Status ▼	Total
Bars	2005	Forecast	1,012,354
		Actual	1,018,550
	2006	Forecast	1,027,665
		Actual	989,874
Cookies	2005	Forecast	1,327,644
		Actual	1,352,814
	2006	Forecast	1,337,854
		Actual	1,334,766
Crackers	2005	Forecast	2,695,533
		Actual	2,682,235
	2006	Forecast	2,685,769
		Actual	2,690,605

Customer (All) ▼

Sum of Qty			
Category ▼	YearNo ▼	Status ▼	Total
Bars			4,048,443
Cookies	2005		2,680,458
	2006	Forecast	1,337,854
		Actual	1,334,766
Crackers	2005		5,377,768
	2006	Forecast	2,685,769
		Actual	2,690,605

Figure 6-4. *The pivot items are visible in the table at the left, and hidden in the table at the right.*

6.17. Using Pivot Fields: Showing Detail for All Items in the Selected Field
Problem

When you select a cell in the outer row field and click the Show Detail button on the PivotTable toolbar, you see the inner row field items for the selected outer row field. The other row field items aren't affected. You'd like to show the details for all items instead of changing each one individually.

Solution

Instead of selecting a single item, select the field before using the Show Details command:

1. Click a field button to select it.

2. On the PivotTable toolbar, click the Show Details button.

6.18. Using Pivot Fields: Showing Details in OLAP-Based Pivot Tables
Problem

Your pivot table is based on an OLAP database. When you select a row field and click the Show Detail button, you get this error message: "You cannot show more detail for that selection. The data displayed is the lowest level of detail available in the source database."

Solution

In OLAP-based pivot tables, when you attempt to show the details for the lowest item in a hierarchy, you'll see the error message. Select an item higher in the hierarchy, and you'll be able to hide and show details.

How It Works

In OLAP-based pivot tables, you can show or hide details for a field if there are items lower in the dimension hierarchy. If there are lower-level items that haven't been displayed, nothing will happen when you click the Hide Details button.

For fields that have lower-level items displayed, you can also select the Hide Levels command. This hides the selected field, as well as any levels above it. For fields that have higher-level items hidden, you can select the Show Levels command. This shows all higher-level items for the selected field.

6.19. Using Pivot Fields: Changing Field Names in the Source Data
Problem

You wanted shorter field names in the pivot table, and changed some column headings in the pivot table's source data. When you refreshed the pivot table, the changed fields disappeared from the pivot table layout. You had to drag them back to the pivot table, and then reapply any field settings that you had previously made.

Solution

Instead of changing the column headings in the source data, create new names for the fields in the pivot table, and the pivot layout won't be affected when you refresh the pivot table. To create a new name for a pivot field, select the cell that contains the pivot field button, and type the new name.

6.20. Using Pivot Fields: Clearing Old Items from Field Dropdown Lists
Problem

You removed old product names from your source data, but they still appear in the Product field dropdown list, even though you've refreshed the pivot table. You want to clear the old names from the dropdown list.

Solution

Follow these steps to manually clear the old items from the dropdown list:

1. If you manually created any groups that include the old items—that is, you selected two or more items, and grouped them—ungroup those items.

2. Drag the pivot field that contains old items out of the pivot table and out of any other pivot tables that use the same pivot cache.

3. On the PivotTable toolbar, click the Refresh button.

4. Drag the pivot field back to the pivot table.

Note When the above steps are followed, the old items are cleared from the pivot cache. However, old items can begin to accumulate again, unless a pivot table option is set programmatically to prevent this. See Chapter 13 for instructions.

6.21. Using Pivot Fields: Changing (Blank) Items in Row and Column Fields
Problem

You want blank cells in the pivot table to contain the text "N/A." You right-clicked a cell in the pivot table and chose Table Options. You checked the For empty cells, show option, and entered **N/A** in the text box beside the option. However, empty cells appear as (Blank) in the row and column fields.

Solution

The For empty cells, show option affects empty cells in the data area, but not the row or column areas. You can manually change those headings by typing over them in the pivot table:

1. Select one of the row or column items that contains the text (Blank).

2. Type **N/A** in the cell, then press the Enter key.

All other (Blank) items in that field will change to N/A.

6.22. Using Pivot Items: Showing All Months for Grouped Dates
Problem

You want to show all 12 months in your pivot table, even though you only have sales data for the first 6 months of the year, with Sales Date grouped by month.

Solution

You can set the Sales Date field to show all possible items:

1. Right-click the Sales Date field button, and choose Field Settings.

2. Add a checkmark to the Show items with no data option, then click OK.

Note If the date field is not grouped, no additional dates will be displayed in the pivot table.

6.23. Using Pivot Items: Showing All Field Items
Problem

Some customers don't make a purchase each month, but you'd like to see a complete list of customers for each month in the pivot table to keep the structure consistent.

Solution

You can set the Customer field to show all items:

1. Right-click the Customer field button, and choose Field Settings.

2. Add a checkmark to the Show items with no data option, then click OK.

■**Note** If the customer name doesn't appear at least once in the source data, it won't be displayed in the pivot table. Add at least one record to the data source with the Customer name in the Customer field. After some real records have been added, you can delete the dummy record.

6.24. Using Pivot Items: Hiding Items with No Data
Problem

You created a calculated item in the pivot table's OrderStatus field, and every salesperson's name now appears in each region. In the PivotTable Field dialog box for the Salesperson field, you unchecked the box for Show items with no data, but it didn't have any effect (see the table at the left in Figure 6-5). You only want the salesperson names to appear for the region in which they're located.

Units		Status ▼	
Region ▼	Rep ▼	Canceled	Sold
East	Jones	151	1749
	Kivell		0
	Parent		288
	Arthur		0
East Total		151	2037
West	Jones		0
	Kivell	118	706
	Parent		0
	Arthur	56	560
West Total		174	1266

Units		Status ▼		
Region ▼	Rep ▼	Canceled	Pending	Shipped
East	Jones	151	830	919
	Parent		173	115
East Total		151	1003	1034
West	Kivell	118	163	543
	Arthur	56	211	349
West Total		174	374	892

Figure 6-5. *In the table at the left, names appear in all regions, due to the calculated item. Hiding Calculated Item (Sold) removes the extra names.*

Solution

When your pivot table includes a calculated item, it may show all the items for some fields, even if Show items with no data is unchecked. Hide the calculated item (see the table at the right in Figure 6-5), and a salesperson's name won't appear in a region where they have no data. If possible, do the calculation in the source data instead of creating a calculated item in the pivot table to avoid the problem of items with no data appearing.

6.25. Using Pivot Items: Ignoring Trailing Spaces When Summarizing Data
Problem

When you apply an AutoFilter on your source data, items with differing trailing spaces, such as "Smith", "Smith ", and "Smith ", show as one entry in the column heading drop-down list. When you add the Customer field to the pivot table, "Smith" and "Smith " show up separately, but you'd like them treated as one item.

Solution

A pivot table doesn't ignore trailing spaces, the way an AutoFilter does. You could add another column to the source table, and use the TRIM worksheet function to remove the extra spaces. For example, do the following if customer names are in column A:

1. Create a new column in the source data, with the heading CustName.

2. In row 2 of the new column, enter the formula

   ```
   =TRIM(A2)
   ```

3. Copy the formula down to the last row of data in the source table.

4. Refresh the pivot table, and add the CustName field to replace the Customer field in the pivot table.

6.26. Using a Pivot Table: Deleting the Entire Table
Problem

You want to remove the pivot table from your workbook, but you can't just delete the worksheet because it contains other data.

Solution

1. Select the cells that contain the pivot table.

2. Choose Edit ➤ Clear ➤ All.

This will remove the pivot table, and all its formatting, from the worksheet. You may see dropdown arrows where the pivot fields were located, but these should disappear when you activate another cell.

6.27. Using a Pivot Table: Changing the Automatically Assigned Name
Problem

When you try to create a pivot table based on an existing pivot table in your workbook, the PivotTable and PivotChart Wizard shows a list of pivot tables with no cell addresses (see Figure 6-6). There are three pivot tables in your workbook, and you want to name them so you can identify them in the list.

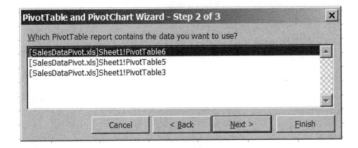

Figure 6-6. *List of PivotTables in Step 2 of the PivotTable and PivotChart Wizard*

Solution

1. Right-click a cell in the pivot table, and choose Table Options.

2. In the Name box, at the top left of the PivotTable Options dialog box, type a name for the pivot table.

3. Click OK to close the PivotTable Options dialog box.

How It Works

When you create a pivot table, it's automatically given the name PivotTable$n$, where n is the next available number in the sequence of pivot tables created during the current session of Excel. For example, if you start Excel and create a pivot table in a workbook that contains a pivot table named PivotTable2, the new pivot table would be named PivotTable1, because it's the first pivot table created in that session of Excel. If you create another pivot table on the sheet that contains PivotTable2, it would be named PivotTable3, because 3 is the next available number on that sheet.

While creating a pivot table, you can click the Options button in Step 4 of the PivotTable and PivotChart Wizard, and type your own name for the pivot table. Or, you can rename the pivot table later, as described in the solution.

The pivot table name can be a maximum of 255 characters, and can include characters such as a question mark, asterisk, or colon. However, it's best to avoid using these characters, as they may cause problems if you plan to do any programming with the pivot table.

CHAPTER 7

■ ■ ■

Updating a Pivot Table

Most pivot tables are based on source data that continues to change; new records or fields may be added to the source, existing records are modified, or the source data is moved to a new location. You want to ensure that your pivot table contains the latest available data, and is correctly connected to the source data.

7.1. Using Source Data: Locating and Changing the Source Excel List

Problem

You've been asked to make some changes to a workbook that contains a pivot table, and you'd like to find the Excel list that was used as the source data. Records have been added to the Excel list, and you want to include them in the pivot table.

Solution

You can locate the source data by using the PivotTable and PivotChart Wizard:

1. Select a cell in the pivot table.

2. On the PivotTable toolbar, choose PivotTable ➤ PivotTable Wizard.

3. Click the Back button.

4. In Step 2 of the PivotTable and PivotChart Wizard, you'll see the range that contains the data.

5. Select the range for the source data, including the new rows and/or columns of data.

■Note When editing the source range for an Excel list, if you like to use keyboard shortcuts to select the range, open the PivotTable and PivotChart Wizard through the PivotTable toolbar, as described in Step 2. If you right-click the pivot table and choose PivotTable Wizard, you won't be able to use the keyboard navigation shortcuts, such as Ctrl+End.

---

6. Click Finish.

How It Works

In Step 2 of the PivotTable and PivotChart Wizard, the data source range is shown in the Range box. This may be a worksheet reference, such as

```
BillingData!$A$1:$J$19
```

or a range name, such as

```
PivotData
```

In most cases, the source range will be visible, and surrounded by a scrolling marquee.

If the source range is not activated, it may be on a hidden worksheet. Follow these steps to unhide the sheet:

1. Close the PivotTable and PivotChart Wizard.

2. Choose Format ➤ Sheet ➤ Unhide.

3. In the list, select the sheet that you want to make visible, and click OK.

■Tip If the sheet name is not on the list of hidden sheets, it may have been hidden programmatically, or removed from the workbook.

If a range name instead of a worksheet reference appears in the Range box and the range is not selected, you can check the name definition:

1. Close the PivotTable and PivotChart Wizard.

2. Choose Insert ➤ Name ➤ Define.

3. In the Names in workbook list, select the name of the pivot table source.

4. In the Refers to box, you'll see the worksheet name on which the range is located.

Tip If the Refers to formula contains #REF! errors, the worksheet, or some of its cells, may have been deleted.

7.2. Using Source Data: Automatically Including New Data

Problem

Your pivot table is based on an Excel list, and you frequently add records to the source data table. You would like the source data range to automatically expand to include any new rows and columns.

Solution

If you frequently add data to the pivot table, you can use a dynamic range as its source. The dynamic range will automatically expand to include the new rows and columns. Follow these steps to create a dynamic range:

1. Select the top-left cell in the source range. This step isn't necessary, but helps you by inserting the cell reference in the name definition.

2. Choose Insert ➤ Name ➤ Define.

3. In the Names in workbook box, type a name for the dynamic range, for example, **PivotSource**.

4. In the Refers to box, type an OFFSET formula that references the selected cell. For example, with cell A1 selected on a worksheet named Pivot, you'd type

   ```
   =OFFSET(Pivot!$A$1,0,0,COUNTA(Pivot!$A:$A),COUNTA(Pivot!$1:$1))
   ```

5. Click the OK button.

Then, change the pivot table's source to the dynamic range:

1. Select a cell in the pivot table.

2. On the PivotTable toolbar, choose PivotTable ➤ PivotTable Wizard.

3. Click the Back button.

4. In the Range box, type the name of the dynamic range, and click Finish.

Tip While in the Range box, to see a list of defined names, choose Insert ➤ Name ➤ Paste. Click on a name to select it, then click OK.

How It Works

The OFFSET function returns a range reference of a specific size, offset from the starting range by a specified number of rows and columns. The function has three required arguments (shown in bold font), and two optional arguments:

`=OFFSET(`**`reference,rows,columns,`**`height,width)`

In our example:

`=OFFSET(Pivot!$A$1,0,0,COUNTA(Pivot!$A:$A),COUNTA(Pivot!$1:$1))`

the returned range starts in cell A1 on the worksheet named Pivot. It is offset zero rows and zero columns. The height of the range is determined by counting the cells that contain data in column A of the Pivot worksheet:

`COUNTA(Pivot!$A:$A)`

The width of the range is determined by counting the cells that contain data in row 1 of the Pivot worksheet:

`COUNTA(Pivot!$1:$1)`

This creates a dynamic range, because if rows or columns are added, the size of the range in the defined name will increase.

Caution This technique will not work if there are other items in row 1 or column A of the Pivot worksheet. Those items would be included in the count, and would falsely increase the size of the source range.

7.3. Using Source Data: Automatically Including New Data in an External Data Range

Problem

Your pivot table is based on an external data range in the same workbook as the pivot table. As new records are added to the external database, they appear in the external data range when it's refreshed. However, the new records don't appear in the pivot table.

Solution

When you import external data to an Excel worksheet, using Data ➤ Import External Data ➤ New Web Query (or New Database Query), a named range is created for the imported data. If you base the pivot table on this named range, it will expand automatically as new records are added, and the pivot table will contain all the data.

1. To see the name of the range, right-click a cell in the external data range, and choose Data Range Properties. The name is at the top of the dialog box.

2. Close the External Data Range Properties dialog box.

3. Choose Insert ➤ Name ➤ Define, and find the external range name in the list.

■**Note** Any spaces in the external data range name will be replaced by underscore characters.

---

4. To the right of the name, you'll see the worksheet name, indicating that it's a sheet-level name. To refer to this name from other worksheets, you'll need to include the sheet name, for example:

```
Sheet1!My_Web_Query
```

5. To base the pivot table on this range, go to Step 2 of the PivotTable and PivotChart Wizard, and type the range name, including the sheet name, in the Range box.

7.4. Using Source Data: Moving the Source Excel List

Problem

Your pivot table is based on an Excel list in another workbook. Using Windows Explorer, you copied the two workbooks to your laptop so you could work at home, and when you tried to refresh the pivot table, you got an error message: "Cannot open PivotTable source file…"

Solution

You can reconnect the pivot table to the Excel list, in its new location:

1. Open the file that contains the source data.

2. Switch to the file that contains the pivot table.

3. On the PivotTable toolbar, choose PivotTable ➤ PivotTable Wizard.

4. Click the Back button to get to Step 2.

5. On the Window menu, select the workbook that contains the source data.

6. Select the range for the source data.

7. Click Finish.

Note When you copy the files back to your desktop computer, you'll have to follow the same steps to reconnect them.

How It Works

When you create a pivot table that's based on a database in another workbook, and that workbook is in a different folder, the folder path is stored as part of the source range. When you copy the files to a different computer, or move the database file to a different folder, the pivot table can't connect to it.

To prevent this problem, create and save the pivot table file in the same folder as the database file. Then, you can move the two files to any other location, and when refreshing, the pivot table will look for the database in its current folder.

7.5. Using Source Data: Changing the Source Excel List

Problem

Your pivot table is based on an Excel list in the same workbook as the pivot table. You want to change the source to a table in another workbook.

Solution

Follow these steps to change the source to an Excel list in a different workbook:

1. Open the workbook that contains the Excel list to which you want to connect.

2. Select a cell in the pivot table, and on the PivotTable toolbar, choose PivotTable ➤ PivotTable Wizard.

3. Click the Back button to get to Step 2.

4. On the Window menu, select the workbook that contains the new source data.

5. Select the range for the source data, and the Range reference will be created, including the workbook name, for example:

    ```
    [NewData.xls]Sheet1!$A$1:$J$18
    ```

6. If you select a named range in the other workbook, the name won't be shown in the Range reference, so you can modify the reference to include it. For example, if the workbook contains a sheet-level range named PivotRange, you'd type

    ```
    [NewData.xls]Sheet1!PTRange
    ```

    For a workbook-level range named PivotRange, you'd remove the square brackets and the sheet reference, and type

    ```
    NewData.xls!PivotRange
    ```

7. Click Finish.

Note The workbook that contains the source data can be opened or closed when you're using or refreshing the pivot table. However, if the reference is to a dynamic range in the other workbook, that workbook must be open in order to refresh the pivot table.

7.6. Using Source Data: Locating the Source Access File

Problem

You inherited a pivot table that's based on a Microsoft Access query. When you click the Get Data button in Step 2 of the PivotTable and PivotChart Wizard, and the Query Wizard opens, you can see the list of tables that are in the source database. However, you can't see the name of the Access file, or tell which table was used to create the pivot table.

Solution

You may be able to find the Access filename and path in Microsoft Query:

1. Right-click a cell in the pivot table, and choose PivotTable Wizard.

2. Click the Back button, then click the Get Data button.

3. If the message "This query cannot be edited by the Query Wizard" appears, click OK.

Tip If the Query Wizard opens, click Cancel, then click Yes, when prompted, to edit the query in Microsoft Query.

---

4. In Microsoft Query, click the SQL button.

5. The last line in the SQL string should start with FROM, and list the database name and path, and the name of the table or query that was used as the source.

6. Click OK to close the SQL dialog box.

7. Choose File ➤ Cancel and Return to Microsoft Office Excel.

8. Click the Cancel button to close the PivotTable and PivotChart Wizard.

7.7. Using Source Data: Trying to Change an OLAP Source

Problem

Your pivot table is based on an OLAP cube, and you would like to change the source. When you go into the PivotTable and PivotChart Wizard, the Back button isn't available, so you can't change the source.

Solution

You can't manually change the source if the pivot table is based on an OLAP cube. Create a new pivot table using the new source data, or programmatically change the data source for the existing pivot table.

7.8. Using Source Data: Changing the Data Source Name File

Problem

Your pivot table is based on an Access query, and it works well on your desktop computer. You copied the Excel file and Access file onto your laptop computer. You also copied the Data Source Name (.dsn) file from the C:\Program Files\Common Files\ODBC\Data Sources directory, and used Notepad to modify it so it refers to the database in the C:\DATA directory on your laptop (see Figure 7-1). However, you can't refresh the database and get the error message that the file is not found.

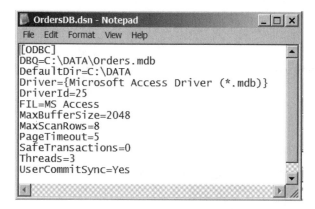

Figure 7-1. *Modify the data source name file in Notepad.*

Solution

Changing the DSN file will affect new pivot tables that are created using that data source, but it won't update the connection for existing pivot tables.

To connect the existing pivot table to the database in its new location, follow the steps described next, in Section 7.9.

7.9. Using Source Data: Changing the Source Access File

Problem

You created a pivot table from an Access query, and the Access file has been moved to a different directory. When you tried to refresh the pivot table, you got the error message "ODBC Microsoft Access Driver Login Failed: Could not find file 'C:\Data\SalesDB.mdb'." You'd like to reconnect the pivot table to the database.

Solution

You can change the connection programmatically, and in some cases you can use the following technique to manually change the source database:

1. Right-click a cell in the pivot table, and choose PivotTable Wizard.

2. Click the Back button, and click the Get Data button.

3. In the error message, click the OK button, and the Login dialog box should appear.

4. Click the Database button.

5. In the Select Database dialog box, select the drive and directory that contain the database file, then select the database file.

6. Click OK to close the Select Database dialog box, then click OK to close the Login dialog box.

7. Microsoft Query should open.

■**Note** If your settings are to use Query Wizard, an error message will appear that says, "This query cannot be edited by the Query Wizard." Click the OK button, and Microsoft Query will open. Then click OK to close the error message "Could not find file…"

---

8. Click the SQL button on the toolbar.

9. In the FROM line of the SQL string, change the path to the new path. For example, if the Access file has been moved to the DataNew directory, you'd type

```
FROM `C:\DataNew\SalesDB`.SalesDB SalesDB
```

■**Note** The SQL statement should contain grave symbols (`) at the start and end of the file path. Leave these in the string, or type them using the ` key on your keyboard.

---

10. Click OK to close the SQL dialog box.

11. Choose File ➤ Return Data to Microsoft Office Excel.

12. In the PivotTable and PivotChart Wizard, click the Finish button.

7.10. Using Source Data: Changing the Source for a Shared Cache

Problem

You created a pivot table based on an Access query, then created several other pivot tables, using the first pivot table as the source. You added a new field to the Access query, and in the first pivot table, used the Get Data button in the PivotTable and PivotChart Wizard to add that field to the pivot table's query. However, the new field didn't show up in the field list for any of the pivot tables that were based on the first pivot table.

Solution

When you create a pivot table, Excel stores a copy of the source data in a memory area called a pivot cache. When you created a pivot table based on another pivot table, the pivot tables shared the same pivot cache. When you changed the query for the first pivot table, it created a new pivot cache for that pivot table, while the second pivot table continued to use the first pivot cache.

You can manually connect each of the secondary pivot tables to the new pivot cache for the first pivot table, or use programming to change the pivot caches for the existing pivot tables.

Follow these steps to manually connect the secondary pivot tables to the new pivot cache:

1. Right-click a cell in a pivot table for which you want to change the data source.

Tip You may find it helpful to rename the source pivot tables before you begin so they're easier to identify in a long list of pivot tables.

---

2. Choose PivotTable Wizard.

3. Click the Back button twice to return to Step 1.

4. Under the Where is the data that you want to analyze? heading, select Another PivotTable report or PivotChart report.

5. Click Next, and in Step 2, select the pivot table that you want to use as the source.

6. Click Finish.

7.11. Using Source Data: Changing the Source CSV File

Problem

You created a pivot table from a CSV file, and want to change the source to a different CSV file. In the PivotTable and PivotChart Wizard, you go back to Step 2 and click the Get Data button, but it doesn't let you select a new file. Instead, you see an error message: "This query cannot be edited by the Query Wizard." Then, Microsoft Query opens, with nothing in it. The pivot table is quite complex, and you'd rather not start from scratch.

Solution

You can create a new query, based on the new CSV file, then use that query in the existing pivot table:

1. In a new Excel file, create a pivot table that's based on the new CSV file, and in the last step of the Query Wizard, click the Save Query button.

2. Save the new Query, click Finish. Then click Finish to exit the PivotTable and PivotChart Wizard and close the new Excel file without saving it.

3. In the existing pivot table, right-click a cell, and choose PivotTable Wizard.

4. Click the Back button, then click the Get Data button.

5. Click OK to close the "This query cannot be edited by the Query Wizard" error message.

6. In Microsoft Query, click OK to close the "The Microsoft Jet database engine could not find the object..." message.

7. Choose File ➤ Open.

8. Select your new CSV query, and click Open.

9. Choose File ➤ Return Data to Microsoft Office Excel.

10. In the PivotTable and PivotChart Wizard, click Finish.

7.12. Refreshing When a File Opens

Problem

Your pivot table source data changes frequently, and you want to ensure that the pivot table is updated as soon as the file opens.

Solution

You can set a pivot table option to refresh the pivot table automatically:

1. Right-click a cell in the pivot table, and choose Table Options.

2. Under Data options, add a checkmark to Refresh on open.

3. Click OK to close the PivotTable Options dialog box.

■Tip To stop a long refresh, as the file opens press the Esc key.

7.13. Preventing a Refresh When a File Opens

Problem

Your pivot table is set to refresh when the file opens, but you occasionally want to open the file without having it refresh.

Solution

You can't manually override the Refresh on open setting. If the pivot table is based on an external source, you may be able to stop the refresh by pressing the Esc key. For other pivot tables, you could open the file programmatically, with events disabled.

7.14. Refreshing Every 10 Minutes

Problem

You frequently add data to your Excel list, and would like the pivot table that's based on the Excel list to refresh automatically every 10 minutes. However, when you right-click the pivot table and choose Table Options, the Refresh every n minutes option is disabled.

Solution

The Refresh every n minutes option in the PivotTable Options dialog box is only available for pivot tables that are based on external data sources. For pivot tables that are based on an Excel list in the same workbook, you can use programming to automatically refresh the pivot table.

7.15. Refreshing All Pivot Tables in a Workbook

Problem

There are several pivot tables in your workbook, and you want to refresh all of them at the same time instead of refreshing each pivot table individually.

Solution

To refresh all the pivot tables in the active workbook at the same time, display the External Data toolbar, and click the Refresh All button.

Note Using the Refresh All command will also refresh all external data ranges in the active workbook, and affects both visible and hidden worksheets.

Adding the Refresh All Button to the PivotTable Toolbar

You can add the Refresh All button to the PivotTable toolbar:

1. Dock the PivotTable toolbar at one of the sides of the Excel window.

2. Click the Toolbar Options arrow at the end of the toolbar.

3. Select Add or Remove Buttons ➤ Pivot Table.

4. Click Refresh All to select it (a checkmark will appear beside each selected button).

5. Click outside the list to close it.

7.16. Reenabling the Refreshing External Data Message

Problem

When you refresh a pivot table that's based on an external data source, you see a message that says, "Refreshing data uses a query to import external data into Excel, but queries can be designed to access confidential information and possibly make that information available to other users, or to perform other harmful actions. If you trust the source of this file, click OK."

At the bottom of the message is the Don't show this message again check box. You checked the box, and no longer see the message, but you'd like to reenable it.

Solution

When you check the Don't show this message again check box, an entry is created in the Windows Registry. You can change the entry to reenable the message.

■**Caution** If you decide to modify the Microsoft Windows Registry, as described next, make a backup copy of the Registry first, and be sure that you know how to restore the Registry if there's a problem. You'll find information on using the Windows Registry in the Microsoft Knowledge Base article "Description of the Microsoft Windows Registry," at http://support.microsoft.com/kb/256986/.

1. On the Windows Taskbar, click the Start button, and then choose Run.

2. In the Open box, type **regedit**, and click OK.

3. Expand HKEY_CURRENT_USER | Software | Microsoft | Office | 11.0 | Excel.

4. Click Options, and in the right pane, select the RefreshAlert option.

5. Choose Edit ➤ Modify.

6. In the Value data box, change the 0 to a 1 (0 sets the RefreshAlert option to Off, and 1 sets the RefreshAlert option to On).

7. Click OK to close the Edit DWORD Value dialog box.

8. Choose File ➤ Exit to close the Registry Editor.

7.17. Problems Obtaining Data When Refreshing

Problem

When you try to refresh your pivot table that's based on an Access query, you get the error message "Problems obtaining data" and you don't know what's causing the problem.

Solution

Usually this error occurs if the query has no data. There may be an error in the Access data, or none of the records match the query criteria. Check the source data to see if there's a problem.

7.18. Stopping a Refresh in Progress

Problem

You clicked the Refresh button to update your pivot table. The refresh is taking a long time to run, and you want to stop it so you can work on something else in the workbook and then run the refresh later.

Solution

To stop a refresh, press the Esc key on the keyboard.

If a refresh is running as a background query, you can double-click the Refresh indicator on the Status bar (see Figure 7-2). In the External Data Refresh Status dialog box, click the Stop Refresh button, then close the dialog box.

Figure 7-2. *Refresh indicator on the Status bar*

7.19. New Data Doesn't Appear When Refreshing an OLAP Cube

Problem

You know that new records have been added to the database, but when you refresh your pivot table, which is based on an OLAP cube, the new data doesn't appear.

Solution

If you're using an offline cube, make sure it's still able to connect to the source database.

7.20. Refreshing an OLAP Cube Causes Client Safety Options Error Message

Problem

You created an OLAP-based pivot table in an older version of Excel. When you open it in Excel 2003 and try to refresh it, you get the error message "Client Safety options do not allow pass through statements to be issued to the data source."

Solution

This error occurs if you have an OLAP cube in which you opted to rebuild the cube every time the report is opened. To stop the message from appearing when the file opens, you can add a new setting to the Windows Registry.

The steps for this are outlined in the Microsoft Knowledge Base article "You Receive an Error When You Create an OLAP Cube-Based PivotTable in Excel 2003," at `http://support.microsoft.com/default.aspx?id=887297`.

▓**Caution** If you decide to modify the Windows Registry, as described in the Knowledge Base article, follow the instructions carefully, and observe the warnings to back up the Registry first, as well as the security cautions.

7.21. Refreshing Pivot Tables with the Same Pivot Cache

Problem

You created a pivot table that's based on another pivot table in the same workbook. You're not sure if you have to refresh each one separately, or if refreshing one will automatically refresh the other.

Solution

If you refresh either of the pivot tables, the other pivot table will be automatically refreshed. Also, if you set the Refresh on open option for either table, both pivot tables will be refreshed when the file opens. If you would prefer that the pivot tables refresh independently, you can create another pivot table based on the same source data, instead of basing it on the first pivot table.

▓**Tip** If a pivot table that's based on another pivot table no longer updates when the first pivot table is refreshed, a new pivot cache may have been accidentally created for one of the pivot tables.

7.22. Refreshing Part of a Pivot Table

Problem

It takes a long time to refresh your pivot table. You want to refresh one field in your pivot table where you know the source data has changed and leave the rest of the data as is, or import the new records but not refresh all the existing ones.

Solution

You can't refresh only part of a pivot table, or just add the new data to the pivot cache. When you refresh the pivot table, the entire pivot table will be affected.

7.23. Enabling Automatic Refresh

Problem

Your pivot table is based on an Access query, and you set the pivot table to refresh on open. Every time the file opens, you get a message that asks you to disable or enable automatic refresh. Even though you selected Enable Automatic Refresh, you continue to see the message when the file opens.

Solution

When you click the Enable Automatic Refresh button, you're permitting the refresh on open to occur. If you select Disable Automatic Refresh, it prevents the refresh on open, but you can still refresh the pivot table manually at any time while the file is open.

To stop the message from appearing when the file opens, you can add a new setting to the Windows Registry. The steps for this are outlined in the Microsoft Knowledge Base article "You Are Prompted to Enable Automatic Refresh When You Open a Workbook in Excel," at http://support.microsoft.com/default.aspx?id=248204. Using a QuerySecurity setting of 2 will stop the message from appearing, and will automatically refresh the pivot table on opening.

Caution If you decide to modify the Windows Registry, as described in the Knowledge Base article, follow the instructions carefully, and observe the warnings to back up the Registry first.

7.24. Refreshing a Pivot Table on a Protected Sheet

Problem

You protected the worksheet that contains your pivot table, and under the Allow all users of this worksheet to list, you added a checkmark to Use Pivot Tables. However, the Refresh button is disabled, and you can't refresh the pivot table.

Solution

The worksheet must be unprotected before you can refresh the pivot table. You can do this manually, or use programming to unprotect the sheet, refresh the pivot table, and then protect the sheet.

7.25. Refreshing Automatically When Data Changes

Problem

You would like to force the pivot table to automatically refresh when the data has changed.

Solution

There's no setting you can change to make this happen. If the pivot table is based on an Excel list, you can use event programming to automatically update the pivot table when the data changes.

7.26. Refreshing When Two Tables Overlap

Problem

You have two pivot tables on the same worksheet and want to stop the error message about overlapping pivot tables.

Solution

You could store each pivot table on a separate worksheet, then use multiple windows in the workbook to view them simultaneously:

1. To create a new window in the active workbook, choose Window ➤ New Window.

2. To view both windows simultaneously, choose Window ➤ Arrange.

3. Select Tiled, and add a checkmark to Windows of active workbook.

7.27. Refreshing Creates an Error Message After Fields Are Deleted

Problem

You cleared the heading cells for a few columns in the source data table for your pivot table. You weren't using the fields in the pivot table, and wanted to clean up the source data. Now, when you try to refresh the pivot table, you see the error message "The PivotTable field name is not valid. To create a PivotTable report, you must use data that is organized as a list with labeled columns. If you are changing the name of a PivotTable field, you must type a new name for the field."

Solution

Instead of clearing the cell contents, delete the entire column. Then, the column will be removed from the source data range, and you won't see the error when you try to refresh the pivot table. If you leave empty cells in the heading row, Excel sees them as invalid field names, and won't let you refresh the pivot table.

7.28. Refreshing Pivot Tables After Queries Have Been Executed

Problem

When you use the Refresh All button on the External Data toolbar, your pivot tables are refreshed before your queries for external data have run. You want to pause the pivot cache refresh until after the queries have been executed.

Solution

You can change a setting for the external data range:

1. Right-click a cell in the external data range.

2. Select Data Range Properties.

3. Remove the checkmark from Enable background refresh, then click OK.

7.29. Refreshing Creates a Too Many Row or Column Items Error Message

Problem

Your pivot table is based on an Access query, and when you try to refresh the data you get an error message that says, "Microsoft Excel cannot make this change because there are too many row or column items. Drag at least one row or column field off the pivot table, or to the page position." You didn't have this problem last week.

Solution

If data has been added to the database, the number of unique items may have increased. A field that fit in the column area last week may now exceed the number of columns available in Excel. Try moving one or more of the fields to the page area, or move a column field to the row area. Then, try the refresh again.

7.30. Refreshing a Scenario Pivot Table

Problem

You used the Tools ➤ Scenarios command to create a scenario that stores the marketing and finance sales forecasts for the upcoming year. In the Scenario Manager, you clicked the Summary button to open the Scenario Summary dialog box, as shown in Figure 7-3, and created a scenario PivotTable report.

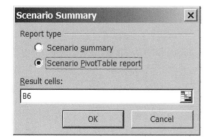

Figure 7-3. *Create a scenario PivotTable report in the Scenario Manager.*

When you select a cell in the pivot table that was created, some buttons are available on the PivotTable toolbar, but the Refresh button is disabled.

Solution

The scenario PivotTable report has very limited functionality, and can't be refreshed. To see a summary of the current values in the scenarios, you can open the Scenario Manager and create a new version of the pivot table.

How It Works

The data for the scenario PivotTable report's pivot cache is a snapshot of the values in each of the scenarios, and is similar to a pivot table based on multiple consolidation ranges. The names of users who created scenarios appear in a dropdown list in the page area. Scenario names appear as items in the row area, and results cells appear as items in the data area (see Figure 7-4).

	B	C	D	E	F
	Dept,Forecast by	(All) ▼			
		Result Cells ▼			
	Dept,Forecast ▼	Profit_Q1	Profit_Q2	Profit_Q3	Profit_Q4
	Finance	750,000	450,000	1,000,000	1,750,000
	Marketing	1,450,000	1,450,000	1,700,000	2,200,000

PivotTable ▼ 閣 🔛 ⁼🗊 ⁼🗊 ! 🖽 🖽 🖽 🖽 🖽 🖽

Figure 7-4. *The scenario PivotTable report with a disabled Refresh button*

Tip To make the scenario PivotTable report easier to understand, you can name the ranges that contain the input cells and results cells. These names, instead of the cell references, will appear in the pivot table field buttons.

CHAPTER 8

Securing a Pivot Table

If other people have access to your pivot table, you may want to disable some of the features, address privacy concerns, monitor access to protected data sources, or prevent users from making some changes. Some pivot table security settings require programming, and are discussed in Chapter 13. Other settings can be made manually, and are explained here.

In Excel, you can protect a file with a password when saving it. You can also password protect a workbook's structure and windows, as well as its worksheet contents. The Microsoft Office 2003 Editions Security Whitepaper (www.microsoft.com/technet/prodtechnol/office/office2003/operate/o3secdet.mspx) discusses security threats that exist and security technologies available in Excel, and other Office programs. The whitepaper describes security threats such as exposure of confidential data, viruses, and malicious code. It outlines the security features available in Office, including digital signatures, file protection, personal data removal, Information Rights Management, and creating security settings.

As with other Excel security features, a knowledgeable user can circumvent most PivotTable protection by using tools, such as password crackers, that are readily available on the Internet. Applying Excel security features will deter novice users, and can help prevent accidental errors or deletions, but may not thwart a determined malicious attack.

8.1. Using a Password-Protected Data Source

Problem

Your pivot table is based on an external data source that is password protected. When you open the Excel file and refresh the pivot table, a Login dialog box appears, in which you have to enter your login name and password. You want to use the pivot table without entering the password every time.

Solution

You can change the PivotTable options to store the password with the pivot table:

1. Right-click a cell in the pivot table, and choose Table Options.

2. Under External data options, add a checkmark to Save password, then click OK.

■Caution If you save the password with the pivot table, it will be visible in the pivot table's connection string, so security concerns may deter you from using this option. See the Notes section of this problem for information on viewing the connection string.

Notes

To view the pivot table's connection string, you can use programming, or, if the pivot table was created from an OLE DB data source, the connection string may be visible in the Edit OLE DB Query dialog box.

Follow these steps to open the Edit OLE DB Query dialog box:

1. Select a cell in the pivot table.

2. Choose Data ➤ Import External Data ➤ Edit Query.

3. In the Edit OLE DB Query dialog box (see Figure 8-1), the connection string, command type, and command text can be viewed and edited.

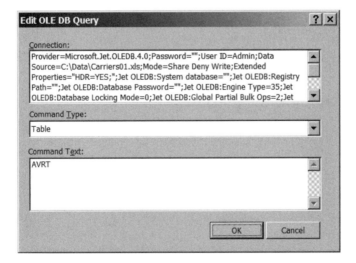

Figure 8-1. *View or edit strings in the Edit OLE DB Query dialog box.*

8.2. Using a Data Source: No Prompt for Password with OLAP Cube

Problem

Your pivot table is based on an offline OLAP cube that you created using the OLAP cube wizard from a secured database. To protect the confidential data in the cube, you want to prompt the user to enter a password in order to use the cube. Currently, the cube is not password protected, and users can select the cube from another Excel workbook and view the current data in the OLAP cube. The database password isn't required until users try to refresh the pivot table.

Solution

When you create an OLAP cube in Excel using the OLAP cube wizard, you can't set a password for the offline OLAP cube. You could protect the cube file by storing it in a secured network folder. Or, in Step 3 of the OLAP cube wizard, choose to rebuild the cube when the report is opened instead of saving a cube file (see Figure 8-2).

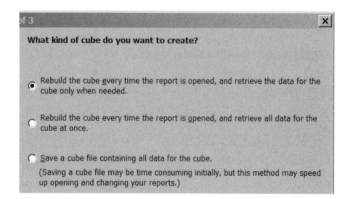

Figure 8-2. *Choose the option to rebuild the cube when the report is opened.*

8.3. Using a Data Source: Access Database with User-Level Security

Problem

Your Access database is protected by user-level security, so you can assign users to groups, and control who has access to the database objects and data. Securing the database creates a workgroup file, with an .mdw extension, where each user is identified by a unique identification code.

You are trying to create a pivot table based on a table in the Access database, but you get the error message "You do not have the necessary permissions to use the 'C:\Data\ SalesDataNew.mdb' object. Have your system administrator or the person who created this object establish the appropriate permissions for you." You have full permissions to the database, and entered a valid user name and password, but still get the error.

Solution

You need to configure a data source so it uses the correct workgroup file. By default, the data source will use the system.mdw workgroup file that's shipped with Access.

To create a data source for the secured Access file, follow these steps:

1. Choose Data ➤ PivotTable and PivotChart Report.

2. Select External data source, and click the Next button.

3. Click the Get Data button.

4. In the Choose Data Source dialog box, select New Data Source and click OK.

5. Type a name for the secured data source, for example, **Secured Sales Database**.

6. From the dropdown list of drivers, select the Microsoft Access driver.

7. Click the Connect button.

8. In the ODBC Microsoft Access Setup dialog box, click the Select button.

9. Select the secured database and click OK.

10. In the System Database section, select Database, and click the System Database button.

11. Select the workgroup file for the secured database, and click OK.

12. Click OK to close the ODBC Microsoft Access Setup dialog box.

13. Click OK to close the error message "Not a valid account name or password."

14. In the Login dialog box, enter a valid login name and password, and click OK.

15. Click OK to close the Create New Data Source dialog box.

16. Click OK to close the Choose Data Source dialog box.

17. In the Query Wizard, or Microsoft Query, create your query, then complete the PivotTable and PivotChart Wizard.

How It Works

To open an Access file that has user-level security, you need to use the workgroup file for that database. This file, with an .mdw extension, is created when user-level security is added to the database, and contains the valid user ID and password information. The previous technique enters the workgroup file information into the DNS file, and that DNS file is used as the data source for the database.

8.4. Protection: Preventing Changes to a Pivot Table

Problem

You want to prevent users from making any changes to the pivot table. They should be able to view the pivot table, but not change the selected items, type over any of the field names, or rearrange the layout. However, you want users to be able to make changes to data and formulas in other areas of the worksheet.

Solution

If you protect the worksheet without enabling pivot table use, or if you share the workbook, users won't be able to modify the pivot table.

Protecting the Worksheet

When protecting a worksheet, prepare the sheet first by unlocking cells where changes can be made. Then, turn on the worksheet protection.

To prepare the sheet, follow these steps:

1. Select any cells in which users will be allowed to make changes.

2. Choose Format ➤ Cells.

3. On the Protection tab, remove the checkmark from Locked. If some selected cells are currently locked, and others are unlocked, the check box will contain a gray checkmark. Click once in the check box to add a black checkmark, then click again to clear the check box (see Figure 8-3).

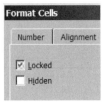

Figure 8-3. *The Locked check box contains a gray checkmark if some selected cells are currently locked and others are unlocked.*

4. Click OK to close the Format Cells dialog box.

Now, to protect the worksheet, do the following:

1. Choose Tools ➤ Protection ➤ Protect Sheet.

2. If desired, enter a password. If you don't enter a password, the worksheet will be protected, but can be unprotected simply by choosing Tools ➤ Protection ➤ Unprotect Sheet.

3. Remove the checkmark from Use PivotTable reports, and check the items that you want enabled on the protected worksheet (see Figure 8-4).

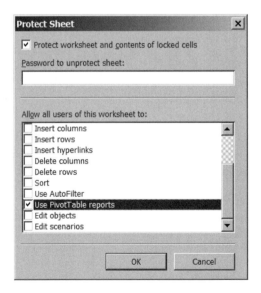

Figure 8-4. *Select items to enable on a protected worksheet.*

4. Click OK and confirm the password, if one was entered.

Sharing the Workbook

Instead of protecting the worksheet, you can share the workbook, which prevents users from changing the pivot table. It also prohibits other activities in the workbook.

1. Choose Tools ➤ Share Workbook.

2. On the Editing tab, add a checkmark to Allow changes by more than one user at the same time. This also allows workbook merging.

3. Click OK, and click OK again to save the workbook if a confirmation message appears.

How It Works

Here's how the two methods prevent changes to the pivot table.

Protecting a Worksheet with Pivot Table Use Not Allowed

If the worksheet is protected, and Use PivotTable reports was not selected in the Allow all users of the worksheet to list, users won't be able to make any changes to the pivot tables on the worksheet. For example, they won't be able to open the dropdown lists on the pivot field buttons, move fields, remove fields, or add fields. The pivot field list will be hidden.

You can create a PivotChart report from a PivotTable report on the protected sheet, but you won't be able to change the PivotChart layout or select an item from its field lists. You will be able to change the PivotChart formatting, chart type, and chart options.

Other pivot tables, based on the pivot tables on a protected sheet, will have some features, such as Refresh Data, disabled.

Tip If you use worksheet protection to disable the pivot table, many other features of the worksheet will also be disabled, such as AutoSum, Spelling, Subtotals, and creating or refreshing a pivot table. If these features are required on the worksheet, you may prefer to use programming to protect the pivot table, while leaving the worksheet unprotected.

Sharing a Workbook

If you share a workbook, in order to disable the pivot table, many other features of the workbook will also be disabled, such as creating charts, adding conditional formatting, and deleting worksheets. If these features are required in the workbook, you may prefer to use programming to protect the pivot table instead of sharing the workbook.

The following features are disabled in a shared workbook:

- Creating or changing PivotTable reports

- Creating or changing charts or PivotChart reports

- Creating lists

- Creating data tables

- Inserting or deleting a range of cells

- Deleting worksheets

- Writing, recording, changing, viewing, or assigning macros

- Merging cells or splitting merged cells

- Adding or changing conditional formats

- Adding or changing data validation

- Assigning, changing, or removing passwords

- Protecting worksheets or the workbook

- Creating, changing, or viewing scenarios

- Grouping or outlining data

- Inserting automatic subtotals

- Working with XML data

- Using a data form to add new data

- Adding or changing Excel 4 dialog sheets

- Changing or deleting array formulas

- Inserting or changing pictures or other objects

- Inserting or changing hyperlinks

- Using drawing tools

8.5. Protection: Allowing Changes to a Pivot Table on a Protected Sheet

Problem

You want to allow users to work with your pivot table, but you don't want them to make changes to data and formulas in other areas of the worksheet.

Solution

If you enable pivot table use when protecting the worksheet, users will be able to modify the pivot table.

Preparing the Worksheet

1. Select all the cells in the worksheet.

Tip To select all the cells on a worksheet, press Ctrl+A, or click the Select All button above the Row 1 button.

---

2. Choose Format ➤ Cells.

3. On the Protection tab, add a checkmark to Locked.

Tip If some selected cells are currently locked and others are unlocked, the check box will contain a gray checkmark. Click once in the check box to add a black checkmark (see Figure 8-2).

---

4. Click OK to close the Format Cells dialog box.

Protecting the Worksheet

1. Choose Tools ➤ Protection ➤ Protect Sheet.

2. If desired, enter a password.

3. Add a checkmark to Use PivotTable reports, and any other items that you want enabled on the protected worksheet (see Figure 8-3).

4. Click OK and confirm the password, if one was entered.

How It Works

If the worksheet is protected, and Allow all users of the worksheet to use PivotTable Reports was selected, users will be able to open the dropdown lists on the pivot field buttons, move the fields, remove fields, and add fields. The pivot field list can be shown.

However, even with the Use PivotTable Reports setting turned on, some commands are disabled if the worksheet is protected, including

- Format Report

- PivotTable and PivotChart Wizard

- Refresh Data

- Group and Ungroup

- Table Options

- Show Pages

- Calculated Field

- Calculated Item

- Enable Selection

- Select

Note When enabling PivotTable report use, you can't control which PivotTable features are allowed. If you want to enable some features, such as selecting items from the Pivot field dropdown lists, and disable other features, such as changing the layout, you can use programming, as described in Chapter 13.

8.6. Protection: Refreshing or Creating a Pivot Table

Problem

You protected a worksheet, and in the list of options, added a checkmark to allow all users of the worksheet to use PivotTable reports. However, you can't create a new pivot table, or refresh a pivot table on the worksheet because some buttons on the PivotTable toolbar are disabled.

Solution

When you protect a worksheet and allow users of the worksheet to use PivotTable reports, they're able to work with existing PivotTable reports. They can't create a new PivotTable report on the protected sheet, or refresh existing pivot tables.

Users can create a pivot table in a new worksheet, based on source data in the protected worksheet. To refresh the pivot table, the worksheet owner can temporarily unprotect the worksheet, refresh the pivot table, then protect the sheet.

8.7. Privacy: Preventing Viewing of Others' Data

Problem

Your pivot table contains sales data for several departments. You want to prevent users from seeing data for departments other than their own.

Solution

You can add worksheet protection to prevent users from selecting a different item in the Department page field. However, if the pivot cache contains data, users may be able to view it by circumventing Excel's security features.

You could create a separate data source for each department, and base its pivot table on that source, with each pivot table in a separate workbook. Or, if users need to see the results but do not need to change the pivot table layout, select each department from the page field, then copy the pivot table and paste as values in another workbook.

■**Tip** After pasting the values, choose Edit ➤ Paste Special, and paste the formats from the original pivot table.

8.8. Privacy: Disabling Drill to Details

Problem

Your pivot table is based on sales data for all salespeople. You want to send the workbook to each salesperson, but prevent them from double-clicking on a data cell to see the details for that data.

Solution

You can protect the workbook structure, or set the pivot table option to disable the Drill to Details feature, then protect the worksheet.

To protect the workbook structure, follow these steps:

1. Choose Tools ➤ Protection ➤ Protect Workbook.

2. Add a checkmark to Structure, and if desired, enter a password.

3. Click OK to close the dialog box, and if prompted, confirm the password.

Follow these steps to disable Drill to Details:

1. Right-click a cell in the pivot table, and choose Table Options.

2. Under Data options, remove the checkmark from Enable drill to details.

3. Click OK to close the PivotTable Options dialog box.

4. To protect the worksheet and disable the Table Options command, choose Tools ➤ Protection ➤ Protect Sheet.

5. If desired, enter a password.

6. Check the items that you want enabled on the protected worksheet.

7. Click OK and confirm the password, if one was entered.

■**Caution** Excel worksheet protection can be easily circumvented. If you don't want users to view the underlying data, don't include the data in the pivot table source.

How It Works

When you protect the workbook structure, it prevents sheets from being added, moved, or deleted. The Drill to Details feature works by inserting a new worksheet and listing the detail for the selected item. If a new sheet can't be inserted, the details aren't listed.

8.9. Privacy: Disabling Show Pages

Problem

To reduce the number of sheets in the workbook, you want to prevent users from using the Show Pages feature. They add pages but don't delete them later, and the workbook size is getting too big.

Solution

You can protect the workbook structure, and users won't be able add new sheets.

1. Choose Tools ➤ Protection ➤ Protect Workbook.

2. Add a checkmark to Structure, and if desired, enter a password.

3. Click OK to close the dialog box, and if prompted, confirm the password.

CHAPTER 9

■■■

Pivot Table Limits and Performance

Excel PivotTable reports can summarize large amounts of data, but there are limits to what can go into different areas of the pivot table layout. When you're working with very large databases, performance can suffer, and creating or refreshing a pivot table can be extremely slow. This chapter outlines some of the limits and discusses ways to optimize the PivotTable performance.

9.1. Understanding Limits: 32,500 Unique Items with External Data Source

Problem

Your pivot table is based on a large external database that contains hundreds of thousands of records. You tried to add an OrderID field to the row area of your pivot table, and got the error message "A field in your source data has more unique items than can be used in a PivotTable report. Microsoft Office Excel may not be able to create the report, or may create the report without the data from this field." You'd like to be able to view the OrderID field in the pivot table.

Solution

If there are more than 32,500 unique items in the field, you won't be able to add it to the pivot table's row, column, or page area. It can go into the data area to be summarized.

When using an external database as the source for a pivot table, you can use one or more page fields to limit the data that's retrieved from the source. These page fields are referred to as server page fields. For example, add the Salesperson field to the page area, and select a salesperson's name from the dropdown list. Only their orders will be retrieved from the external database, and the number of unique OrderIDs should be below the 32,500 unique item limit.

■Note This option is not available for OLAP-based pivot tables.

1. Move one or more fields to the page area of the pivot table.

2. Right-click a page field, and choose Field Settings.

3. Click the Advanced button.

4. Under Page field options, select Query external data source as you select each page field item (requires less memory).

5. Leave the checkmark in Disable pivoting of this field (recommended).

■Tip This setting will prevent users from accidentally moving the field to another part of the pivot table, where it could damage the pivot table layout.

6. Click OK to close the PivotTable Field Advanced Options dialog box.

7. Click OK to close the PivotTable Field dialog box.

8. Select an item from the page field dropdown list to see the data for that item in the pivot table.

■Note The (All) option is removed from the page field's dropdown list of items. If (All) was selected in the page field, when Query external data source as you select each page field item is turned on, the first item in the list will be selected after the query runs. If an item is selected in the page field, it will remain selected after the option is turned on.

To regain the ability to show all records, you can turn off the Query external data source as you select each page field item setting:

1. Double-click the page field button.

2. In the PivotTable Field dialog box, click the Advanced button.

3. Under the Page field options, select Retrieve external data for all page field items (faster performance).

4. Click OK to close the PivotTable Field Advanced Options dialog box,

5. Click OK to close the PivotTable Field dialog box.

How It Works

Using the Query external data source as you select each page field item option creates server page fields that restrict the amount of data that's returned from the source database. When you turn this option on, you can no longer select to see all the data from the field but can select only one item at a time. For example, for a Region field, only one region can be selected, and only its records are summarized in the pivot table.

When you select an item from a server page field, Microsoft Query opens and returns the data for the selected page field item. You'll see the Microsoft Query button on the Windows Taskbar, and may see the query progress indicator at the left side of the Excel Status bar. The pivot cache is cleared and then filled with records for the newly selected item. The pivot table is refreshed and shows the current records.

When using this option, it's best to leave on the setting for Disable pivoting of this field, as recommended in the PivotTable Field Advanced Options dialog box. If the page field were moved to another part of the pivot table, the Query external data source setting would be automatically turned off. All the data would be retrieved, and fields with too many unique items would be removed from the pivot table layout.

Using this option may make the pivot table slower when you select a different item in the page field dropdown list. Because it has to retrieve the data from the external source, then display it, it takes longer than changing the item in a normal page field dropdown, where all the data is already available.

An advantage to using the option is that less memory is used, because all the data isn't in the pivot cache. This can make the file size much smaller, even if the data is saved with the pivot table. Also, by returning the data in smaller segments, you can prevent some fields from exceeding the unique item limit, which they might otherwise hit if all the data were returned.

Tip If you apply this setting to a page field in the PivotTable and PivotChart Wizard, as you create the pivot table, the initial setup time for the pivot table may be faster.

9.2. Understanding Limits: 32,500 Unique Items with Excel Data Source

Problem

Your pivot table is based on a large Excel list. You tried to add an OrderID field to the row area of your pivot table, and got the error message "A field in your source data has more unique items than can be used in a PivotTable report. Microsoft Office Excel may not be able to create the report, or may create the report without the data from this field." You can't create server page fields, as described in Section 9.1, because the pivot table source isn't an external database.

Solution

If there are more than 32,500 unique items in the field, you won't be able to add it to the pivot table's row, column, or page area. It can go into the data area to be summarized.

One option is to name the range that contains the Excel list and create the pivot table in a different workbook, using the named list as an external data source. Then, use the server page fields, as described in Section 9.1.

Another option is to use calculations in the source data to split the entries into multiple fields. For example, if there is an eight-digit OrderID number in column A, use LEFT and RIGHT formulas to create two new fields.

1. Create two new columns in the pivot table source list.

2. Add the headings OrderID_A and OrderID_B.

3. In row 2 of the OrderID_A column, enter the formula

   `=LEFT(A2,4)`

4. In row 2 of the OrderID_B column, enter the formula

   `=RIGHT(A2,4)`

5. Copy the formulas down to the last row of data.

6. Refresh the pivot table, and add the new fields to the row or page area. With four digits per field, there would be a maximum of 10,000 unique entries in each field, which is well below the unique item limit.

9.3. Understanding Limits: Only the First 255 Items Displayed

Problem

You tried to add the Sales Date field to the column area of your pivot table, and got a message that said the field exceeds 255 items (see Figure 9-1). You want to show the dates in the column area, not a different area.

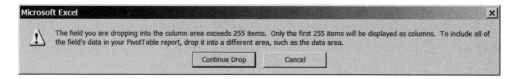

Figure 9-1. *Message displayed when column field items exceed 255 items*

Solution

The 255 items mentioned in the error message refers to the number of columns available to display the items, rather than a pivot table limit. You can add the date field to the column area, and as many dates as possible will be displayed. Then, leave the field as is, or group the dates so the full date range is displayed.

1. Click the Continue Drop button to allow the field to be added to the column area.

2. Click OK to the next message that appears: "The PivotTable report will not fit on the sheet. Do you want to show as much as possible?"

3. As many dates as will fit are displayed in the column area.

4. To group the dates, right-click the Date field button.

5. Choose Group and Show Detail ➤ Group.

Note If the date field contains blank cells, or cells with text, you won't be able to group the dates.

---

6. Choose a time period for grouping. For example, select Days, and set the number of days to 7 to summarize the data in one-week periods.

7. Click OK to close the Grouping dialog box.

How It Works

Date fields often have too many unique values to display in the column area of the pivot table. There are only 256 columns on the Excel worksheet, and at least one column is reserved for the row area, even if there are no row fields currently in the pivot table.

If you add a field to the column area and it has too many items to display, nothing is lost from the pivot table. In most cases, if you move the field to the row area, you can see all the items.

9.4. Understanding Limits: 8,000 Items in a Column Field

Problem

You tried to add the Order ID field to the column area of your pivot table. When you dragged the field onto the column area, the pointer didn't change to the column area shape, as it normally does. When you released the mouse button, you got a warning message that said the field has more than 8,000 items and can't be placed in the column area (see Figure 9-2).

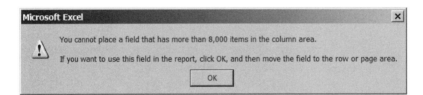

Figure 9-2. *Error message when a column has more than 8,000 items*

Solution

As the warning message suggests, you could place the field in the row or page area of the pivot table instead of the column area.

■**Caution** If the field will cause the row area to exceed its row limit, the placement will fail without a warning message.

If you place the field in the row area, you may be able to group the items to create fewer items than the 8,000 limit, and then move the grouped field to the column area.

Tip If you move the grouped field back to the column area, you can ungroup it, with no error message, even though it exceeds the 8,000-item limit. As many items as will fit will be displayed.

How It Works

When you select a field in the field list, the items in that field are counted. At the bottom of the field list, select Column Area from the dropdown list of areas, and if there are more than 8,000 items in the field, the Add button will be disabled. If there are more than 32,500 items in the field, the Add button may be disabled when you select Column Area, Row Area, or Page Area.

    If you drag a field with more than 8,000 items from the field list to the column area, the pointer, which normally changes to a column area pointer, keeps its rectangular button shape (see Figure 9-3). This indicates that you won't be successful if you try to drop the field in the column area.

Figure 9-3. *Pointer with the rectangular button shape indicating that a field can't be placed in the column area*

9.5. Understanding Limits: Too Many Row or Column Items

Problem

You added more records to your source data, and when you tried to refresh the pivot table, you got the error message "Microsoft Office Excel cannot make this change because there are too many row or column items. Drag at least one row or column field off the PivotTable report or to the page position. Alternatively, right-click a field, and then click Hide or Hide Levels on the shortcut menu." You didn't add any new fields to the source data, or change the pivot table layout, and were able to refresh previously without a problem.

Solution

When new records were added to the source data, they may have created new items in the existing fields, or new combinations of items in a record. For example, new salespeople were hired, or some salespeople sold products they hadn't previously sold. This created too many items for the row or column area of the pivot table.

Follow the instructions in the error message, and move or remove some of the fields. In most cases, it's the column field item limit that's been exceeded, as it is much lower than the row field item limit. Move one or more column fields to the page area, then refresh the pivot table.

Notes

Sometimes the pivot table becomes corrupted as the workbook opens if an item limit has been surpassed, even though the pivot table is not set to refresh on open. You may see an incorrect message that says "One or more PivotTable reports based on external sources have been marked for update on load" (see Figure 9-4).

Figure 9-4. *Message that appears when opening a file with the item limit exceeded*

If you click OK, Excel can usually repair the pivot table. If it's not successful, you may have to create a new PivotTable report, with fewer column fields. If you click Cancel, the repair is usually unsuccessful, and when you try to work with the pivot table, the only response is an error message: "This PivotTable report is not valid."

■**Tip** When working with a large PivotTable report, move column fields with many items to the page area before refreshing the pivot table or closing the workbook.

How It Works

The number of row and column fields that can be added to a PivotTable report is limited only by your computer's memory. However, there are limits to the number of field items that can be placed in the row and column areas. For column field items, the limit is 32,768, and for row field items, the limit is 2^{31} (2 to the power of 31), which is approximately 2.1 billion items.

The total number of items in the column or column area is calculated by multiplying the number of unique items in each field. For example, a pivot table might have the following fields (item count is shown following each field name): Salesperson (10), Region (5), Products (30), Brands (3), and Periods (13).

The total number of items is $10 \times 5 \times 30 \times 3 \times 13 = 58,500$.

Although this number is above the 32,768-item limit, you might be able to place all the fields in the column area, because it's unlikely that all possible combinations are found in the source data. For example, each salesperson probably works in only one region, not five, and each product is sold under one brand, not all three.

Even if each salesperson sells every product in every period, the used combinations would be much lower: $10 \times 1 \times 30 \times 1 \times 13 = 3,900$.

So, although the PivotTable report field items exceed the theoretical limit, Excel counts the actual combinations in the source data, and would allow all the fields to be added to the column area.

■Note In earlier versions of Excel, the theoretical limit was applied, so use of the column area was much more restricted.

9.6. Understanding Limits: Text Truncated in a Pivot Table Cell

Problem

One of the fields in your pivot table's data source contains comments about the sales order. Some of the comments are quite long, and are truncated when they appear in the pivot table. You'd like to see the full comment instead of the shortened version.

Solution

The cell contents of a pivot table are limited to 255 characters. Any characters beyond that limit are truncated. You could add another field in the source data and number the comments. In the pivot table workbook, list the numbered comments on another sheet, where users can view the full comment. In the pivot table, show the comment number and short comment only.

9.7. Understanding Limits: Number of Records in the Source Data

Problem

You want to create a pivot table from a database that contains thousands of records in 20 fields, but don't know if the pivot table would be able to work with that much data.

Solution

There's no fixed maximum on the number of records that the source database can contain, but working with a large database can be slow. For large databases, you can create an OLAP cube that presummarizes some of the data and can be used to build a pivot table in Excel.

In the PivotTable and PivotChart Wizard, if you select External data source in Step 1, you'll have the opportunity to create an OLAP cube from your data source in the final step of the Query Wizard, or in Microsoft Query, where you can choose File ➤ Create OLAP Cube. The OLAP Cube Wizard will guide you through the process.

How It Works

Although there's no fixed limit to the number of records in the source database, creating a PivotTable report from a large external database can result in a very slow pivot table. Also, there are other limits that may affect your work, as shown in Table 9-1.

Table 9-1. *Pivot Table Limits*

Feature	Limit	Note
Pivot Table Size	No fixed limit	The maximum size for the pivot table is controlled by the available memory in your computer, and the other limits, listed below.
Number of Row Fields	No fixed limit	Row field item counts, as listed below, may limit the number of fields you can add. The available memory in your computer may also limit the number of fields that you can add.
Number of Column Fields	No fixed limit	Column field item counts, as listed below, may limit the number of fields you can add. The available memory in your computer may also limit the number of fields that you can add.
Unique Items per Row, Column or Page Field	32,500	You can't drop a field in the column area if the field has more than 8,000 unique items.
Displayed Column Field Items	255	There are only 256 columns in an Excel worksheet, and one is reserved for row headings, so you can't display more than 255 column field items.

Feature	Limit	Note
Total Column Field Items	32,768	Excel calculates the number of potential field item combinations that your pivot table requires, and that number, in theory, can't exceed 32,768. If you try to add column fields that will result in the number being exceeded, you'll see an error message. For more information on this limit, see Section 9.5.
Total Row Field Items	2^31	The limits for row field item combinations, approximately 2.1 billion, is much greater than the column field item limit.

9.8. Improving Performance When Changing Layout

Problem

Using your OLAP database as the source, a pivot table responds very slowly when you add fields to a new pivot table, or move fields to a different area of the pivot table, using the worksheet layout, and you'd like to speed up the process.

Solution

On the PivotTable toolbar, turn off the Always Display Items feature. This hides the row and column fields until you add fields to the data area. Then, when creating a new pivot table, add the page, row, and column fields first, then add fields to the data area.

Follow these steps to modify an existing pivot table:

1. On the PivotTable toolbar, if the Always Display Items button is enabled, click it to turn it off (see Figure 9-5).

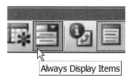

Figure 9-5. *The Always Display Items button on the PivotTable toolbar*

2. In the pivot table, right-click the Data field button and choose Hide.

Note If there is only one data field, the Data field button will show the name of the data field, e.g., Sum of Units. If there are multiple data fields, the field button will have the label "Data".

3. Change the pivot table layout by adding, removing, or moving the pivot fields.

4. Drag the removed data fields back from the pivot field list to the pivot table data area.

If the process is still slow, use the PivotTable and PivotChart Wizard to make layout changes. This method can be faster than the worksheet layout if the source data has a large number of records or multiple data fields.

1. Right-click a cell in the pivot table, and choose PivotTable Wizard.

2. Click the Layout button.

3. Add, remove, or move the pivot fields in the layout diagram.

4. Click OK, then click Finish to return to the worksheet.

Also, use the PivotTable and PivotChart Wizard method if you want to add fields to the pivot table's page area to show one page of data at a time from a large external source. This creates server pages, and is described in Section 9.1.

How It Works

Turning off the Always Display Items feature may have a positive impact on OLAP-based pivot tables, because if items are showing, the OLAP server is queried each time a field is added.

For example, in a pivot table based on an OLAP cube with two data fields, two row fields were moved to a different position in the row area. As shown in Table 9-2, using the PivotTable and PivotChart Wizard method was approximately twice as fast as moving the fields on the worksheet, with the Always Display Items feature turned on.

Table 9-2. *Comparison of Layout Change Methods*

Method	Time
Change layout in PivotTable and PivotChart Wizard:	3:28 minutes
Change layout on worksheet, Always Display Items off:	4:22 minutes
Change layout on worksheet, Always Display Items on:	7:28 minutes

9.9. Improving Performance with the Optimize Memory Option

Problem

Your pivot table is based on an external data source, and you wonder if its speed will improve if you use the Optimize memory option.

Solution

You can turn on the Optimize memory option if you experience insufficient memory errors while working with your pivot table:

1. Right-click a cell in the pivot table, and choose Table Options.

2. Under External data options, add a checkmark to Optimize memory, then click OK.

Otherwise, leave the option turned off, as it has a negative impact on speed.

▧**Note** This option isn't available for OLAP-based pivot tables.

How It Works

The Optimize memory option was introduced in Excel 97 to address memory problems that occurred when creating pivot tables in earlier versions of Excel. When the option is on, Excel queries the external data if the pivot table is refreshed, or the layout is changed, to count the unique items in each field. If there are 256 or fewer items, it can optimize the storage for that field.

As a result, when the option is turned on, refreshing the pivot table is much slower. For example, with a pivot table based on a Microsoft Access query with 30,000 records, the pivot table refreshed in under 3 seconds with the Optimize memory option turned off. With the option turned on, the refresh took more than 10 seconds.

The memory limit has been increased dramatically in Excel 2003, compared to earlier versions—from 128MB in Excel 2002 to 1GB in Excel 2003, so memory errors occur less frequently. The differences are outlined in the Microsoft Knowledge Base article "'Not Enough Memory' Error Messages When You Copy Formulas Over Large Area in Excel," at http://support.microsoft.com/default.aspx?id=313275. For a thorough discussion of Excel's memory limits, see Charles Williams' article, "Out of Memory, Memory Limits, Memory Leaks, Excel Will Not Start," at www.decisionmodels.com/memlimitsc.htm.

9.10. Reducing File Size: Excel Data Source

Problem

Your workbook contains a few pivot tables, and has almost doubled in size, even though you only added a few rows to the Excel list that's the pivot table source. Every time you add a pivot table, the size goes up a few megabytes. You'd like to make the file smaller.

Solution

To reduce the file size, try one of the following options.

Sharing a Pivot Cache

When you create a pivot table, a pivot cache is created, which stores a copy of the source data. If you add another pivot table to the workbook and base it on an existing pivot table in the same workbook, it uses the pivot cache from the first pivot table, which saves memory and reduces the file size.

   If they use the same Excel list as their source data, you can change existing pivot tables so they share the same pivot cache.

▓**Tip** You may find it helpful to rename the source pivot tables before you begin, so they're easier to identify in a long list of pivot tables.

---

1. Right-click a cell in a pivot table for which you want to change the data source.

2. Choose PivotTable Wizard.

3. Click the Back button twice to return to Step 1.

4. Under the heading "Where is the data that you want to analyze?," select Another PivotTable report or PivotChart report.

5. Click Next, and in Step 2, select the pivot table that you want to use as the source.

6. Click Finish.

Changing the Pivot Table Layout

Also, the pivot table layout can have a dramatic effect on the file size. If the pivot table layout is large, the used range is larger, and this can increase the file size. If file size is a concern, move most fields to the page area before closing the workbook to minimize the used range.

Turn Off Save Data with Table Layout

To make the file smaller when saving, you can change a pivot table option so the data isn't saved when the workbook is closed:

1. Right-click a cell in the pivot table, and choose Table Options.

2. Under Data source options, remove the checkmark from Save data with table layout.

3. Click OK to close the PivotTable Options dialog box.

Storing the Excel List in a Separate Workbook

The Excel list on which the pivot tables are based can be stored in a separate workbook. This will reduce the size of the workbook that contains the pivot tables. The Excel list workbook can remain closed when working with the pivot table file, and that will reduce the amount of memory used.

How It Works

When you change a pivot table's data source to another pivot table, it means that the second pivot table uses the same cache as the first pivot table. If no pivot table is using the second pivot cache, that cache is deleted, and the file size is smaller.

When the data isn't saved with the layout, the file size is smaller because the pivot cache isn't being saved, and it reduces the time required to save the workbook. When you open the workbook, you'll have to refresh the pivot table to rebuild the pivot cache when you want to use the pivot table. This will be slower than refreshing a pivot table with a saved cache.

CHAPTER 10

Publishing a Pivot Table

After you create a PivotTable report, you may want to publish the pivot table, its pivot chart, or the entire workbook, on a web page. In Excel, you can create files in HTML format, with or without interactivity. Without interactivity, a PivotTable or PivotChart report can be viewed on a web page, but not manipulated. With interactivity, visitors to the web page can modify the PivotTable or PivotChart report layout, select from the pivot field dropdown lists, and make other changes.

If you choose to add interactivity, an Office Web Component (OWC) is created, based on the Excel worksheet, pivot table, or pivot chart. In order to view or interact with your OWC PivotTable list, visitors to the web page need to have Office 2003 Web Components installed, as described in "How It Works" in Section 10.3.

This chapter will focus on the steps you can take within Excel to prepare and publish the Excel pivot table and pivot chart.

10.1. Publishing a Pivot Table: Understanding HTML

Problem

When you save an Excel file as a web page, it's saved in Web Page format, with an .htm or .html extension. You're not familiar with that format, and would like to learn more about it.

Solution

Files saved as web pages in Excel are saved in HyperText Markup Language (HTML) format. HTML is a language that's used to create web pages. You don't need to know anything about the language to create an HTML file from an Excel file—the format is automatically created for you when you save a file as a web page.

For a good introduction to HTML, see the National Center for Supercomputing Applications (NCSA) article "A Beginner's Guide to HTML," at `http://archive.ncsa.uiuc.edu/General/Internet/WWW/HTMLPrimerP1.html`.

10.2. Publishing Without Interactivity: Preparing the Excel File

Problem

You've been asked to publish your workbook on the company website, so visitors can see the PivotTable report and PivotChart report that summarize the company sales and the source data that's on a different worksheet.

Solution

You can create a web page from your Excel file without interactivity. The web page will contain a static picture of the Excel file contents, in which visitors can view the information but not change it. Prepare the workbook, pivot table, and pivot chart to ensure that visitors can find the information they need, and then save the file as a web page.

Preparing the Workbook

1. Ensure that columns are wide enough to show all the data they contain, and that rows are tall enough. Because the published HTML file is static, users won't be able to adjust the cell width or height.

2. Add any formatting that you want to display on the web page. Some formatting, including the items listed here, is not retained when a noninteractive workbook is published.

   • Rotated text in cells

   • Cell fill pattern

   • Double underline

   • Sheet tab color

   • Cell comment triangles (these are changed to numbers)

3. Give each worksheet a meaningful name, to help visitors navigate through the workbook. For example, change the default name Sheet1 to Sales Data. Even if sheet tabs are turned off in the Tools ➤ Options, View tab, they will be visible on the web page.

4. If you are publishing the entire workbook, delete any unused worksheets so visitors aren't confused by blank sheets. If more than one sheet in the workbook contains data or formatting, all visible sheets will appear in the published workbook. Although you plan to publish the file without interactivity, the sheet tabs in the published workbook can be clicked to view each sheet (see Figure 10-1).

Figure 10-1. *Sheet tabs appear in Internet Explorer when multiple sheets are published.*

Preparing the PivotTable Report

1. Add all required fields to the PivotTable report layout, as visitors won't be able to change the layout.

2. Don't place fields in the page area unless you plan to filter the pivot table data before publishing it. Otherwise, the page fields take up space at the top of the web page, and don't add value to the information presented.

3. Ensure that all columns in the PivotTable report are wide enough to show the data they contain, and that all rows are tall enough.

4. Add any formatting that you want to display in the PivotTable report. For the web version of the PivotTable report, you may want more color than you would use in a printed copy.

Tip To quickly format the PivotTable report so it has impact on the web page, you can select a cell in the PivotTable report, and choose Format ➤ AutoFormat.

Preparing the PivotChart Report

1. Add all required fields to the PivotChart report layout.

2. Don't place fields in the page area unless you plan to filter the data before publishing the chart. Otherwise, the page fields take up space that could be used by the chart's plot area.

3. Hide the PivotChart field buttons to reduce the clutter in the chart.

4. Add a title to the chart to explain its content. If the chart has been filtered, include that information in the title, for example, **Sales – Eastern Region – 2006**.

5. When published, the text on a chart sheet may appear blurred (see Figure 10-2).

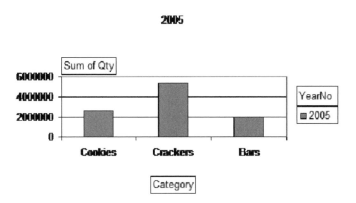

Figure 10-2. *Blurred text in a published PivotChart on the chart sheet*

If possible, move the chart to a regular worksheet, and publish it there. The text quality will be better (see Figure 10-3), and you can easily adjust the size of the chart so it fits on the web page.

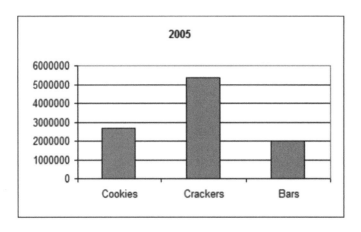

Figure 10-3. *Clear text in a published PivotChart embedded on the worksheet, with the PivotChart fields hidden*

Previewing the Web Page

After preparing the workbook, PivotTable report, or PivotChart report, you can see how it will look on a web page. This technique displays the entire workbook as a web page, with interactive tabs that allow you to view any sheet. If your PivotTable report or PivotTable report is on a worksheet with other data, that data will also be included in the preview. When saving the file as a web page, you can specify which regions you want to publish.

1. Select any cell in the workbook.

2. Choose File ➤ Web Page Preview.

3. Your default web browser will open, with the active sheet in the workbook displayed.

4. If sheet tabs are visible, you can click them to view other sheets.

5. Close the web browser program, and make any adjustments required to the Excel file before publishing.

Publishing the Web Page

After you prepare and preview the web page, you can publish it without interactivity by choosing File ➤ Save as Web Page. For detailed instructions, see Excel's Help.

10.3. Publishing with Interactivity: Pivot Charts and Pivot Tables

Problem

You've been asked to publish your pivot chart and pivot table on the company website, so visitors can change the layout and select items from the pivot field dropdown lists.

Solution

If you publish a pivot table or pivot chart with interactivity, visitors will be able to make changes to the pivot table and pivot chart on the web page, such as adding and removing fields and creating formulas. Office Web Components (OWCs) are created in the HTML file, based on the objects in the Excel file. These will look different than the Excel objects, and have different functionality. Prepare the pivot table and pivot chart to optimize the components that will be created on the web page.

■**Note** If you publish the entire workbook with interactivity, charts won't be included, and PivotTable reports will be static on the worksheet.

Preparing the PivotTable Report

1. Most formatting will be lost when you publish a pivot table with interactivity. However, number formatting will be retained if you use the PivotTable Field settings dialog box, instead of selecting cells in the pivot table to format. To do this, right-click on a pivot table cell, and choose Field Settings.

2. If the worksheet that contains the pivot table or pivot chart is protected, remove the password if one is used. Password-protected sheets can't be published as web pages.

Preparing the PivotChart Report

1. Select a chart type and subtype that best presents the data. Visitors won't be able to change the chart type. The Cone, Cylinder, and Pyramid chart types will be changed to Column charts in the web page. Charts with a Surface chart type will not be loaded on the web page.

2. If there's a data table on the chart, it won't appear in the published pivot chart. You can add value labels to the chart series to display the values, or remind visitors that values will be displayed when they point to a data point on the chart.

Publishing the Web Page

To create an HTML file from your PivotChart and PivotTable report that can be published on a website with interactivity, follow these steps:

1. Select any cell in the workbook.

2. Choose File ➤ Save As Web Page.

3. Select the directory in which you want to store the HTML file.

4. Click the Publish button to open the Publish as Web Page dialog box.

5. Under Item to publish, from the Choose dropdown, select Items on [Name of sheet that contains the PivotChart report].

6. In the list of items, select your PivotChart report.

Note When you publish a pivot chart, the connected pivot table is automatically published on the same web page.

7. Click in the Add interactivity with box to add a checkmark.

8. If you want to add a title to the published page, click the Change button and type a title. The title will appear above the published components.

9. Click OK to close the Set Title dialog box, and the title will be displayed on the Publish As Web Page dialog box, to the left of the Change button.

10. To automatically update the HTML file, if the Excel file is saved, add a checkmark to AutoRepublish every time this workbook is saved.

Tip Select this option if you expect to change the Excel file later and will want to publish the updated version. It will save an updated version of the HTML file without any extra work on your part.

11. To immediately see the results in your browser, add a checkmark to Open published web page in browser.

12. Click the Publish button to save the file.

How It Works

When you publish a pivot table and select the interactivity option, an Office Web Component (OWC) PivotTable list is added to the HTML file. This component has some features similar to those of an Excel PivotTable report, as well as some features that are different.

A folder is also created with the name of the HTML file, followed by _files, that contains files with information about the published file. For example, one of the files in the folder has the same name as the HTML file, followed by a random number and _cachedata.xml. This file contains the source records for the PivotTable list. Upload both the HTML file and the folder when putting the files on your web server.

You can publish the HTML file as created by Excel, or modify it in Microsoft FrontPage or another website-creation software package.

Licensing

To interact with the PivotTable list component on a web page, users must use Microsoft Internet Explorer 5.01 or later, and must have a valid license for Microsoft Office 2003 or for a later version of Microsoft Office that includes the Office 2003 Web Components. Without a license, users are in View-only mode, and can do the following:

- View data

- Print

- Select and scroll

- Use hyperlinks

- Resize a component

- Select sheets in the Spreadsheet component

- Expand or collapse members in a PivotTable list

- Refresh data in a PivotTable list

- Use the About, Help, and Refresh commands

For information on OWC licensing requirements, see the Microsoft Knowledge Base article "General Information About the Licensing and the Use of Office 2003 Web Components," at http://support.microsoft.com/default.aspx?scid=828949.

OWC Features

It's beyond the scope of this book to provide extensive coverage of the OWC PivotTable features, but we'll outline some of the key similarities and differences between the two types of pivot tables.

The OWC PivotTable will contain the page, row, column, and data fields from your Excel PivotTable report. The fields can be moved to a new location, or removed from the pivot table. Click the Field List button in the OWC toolbar to open the field list and add more fields to the pivot table.

The Summary functions for the data fields are those that appeared in the original Excel PivotTable and can't be changed. You can create custom calculations, such as Percent of Row, Calculated Totals, and Calculated Detail Fields.

Items in the row, column, and data areas can be sorted, filtered, and grouped. For example, you can show only the top five customers, or the bottom 10 percent of your products.

▪Note An OWC feature that's not available in Excel's pivot tables is the ability to group by prefix characters. You could use this to group customers by the first letter in their name, or group budget codes by the first four digits. Date fields can be grouped, even if there are blank cells in the field.

Most formatting from the Excel pivot table is lost when the OWC pivot table is created. You can select fields and apply formatting on the web page by using the Commands and Options dialog box, which you open by clicking the button shown in Figure 10-4.

Figure 10-4. *The Commands and Options button on the PivotTable list toolbar*

OWC Toolbar

Selecting a different part of the pivot table can change the buttons that are visible on the OWC toolbar. If you select a Row field button, a Subtotal button appears that lets you toggle the Subtotals on and off. An AutoCalc button lets you select a Summary function for the selected field. Select a cell in the data area, and the Show As button is available, which provides a list of options for viewing the data, such as Percent of Grand Total. These options include Percent of Parent Row, and Percent of Parent Column, which calculate the percent an item comprises of the Parent (outer) field's subtotal.

10.4. Publishing: Interactive Pivot Table Blocked

Problem

You published a pivot table with interactivity, but some visitors to the web page are blocked from using it. They see the shell of the pivot table but none of the data. In the center of the pivot table, there's a message that says, "No Details: The query could not be processed: The data provider didn't supply any further error information" (see Figure 10-5).

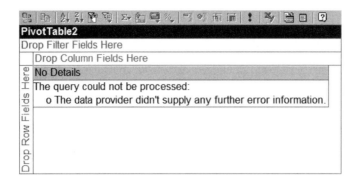

Figure 10-5. *The interactive PivotTable is blocked from use.*

Solution

Security features in the Internet browser may block use of the Office Web Components (OWCs) PivotTable list. If using Internet Explorer 6.0, visitors can add your site to their list of trusted sites with a customized security level, and the pivot table would work correctly. Follow these steps to add a site to the list of trusted sites.

■**Caution** Changing the security setting in the Internet browser can put your computer at risk.

---

1. In Internet Explorer, choose Tools ➤ Internet Options.

2. On the Security tab, under Select a Web content zone to specify its security settings, select Trusted sites.

3. Click the Sites button to open the Trusted sites dialog box.

4. If the site is not a secure site, remove the checkmark from the Require server verification (https:) for all sites in this zone check box.

5. In the Add this Web site to the zone: box, type the name of the website, for example, **www.Apress.com**.

6. Click the Add button, then click OK to close the Trusted sites dialog box.

7. Under Security level for this zone, click the Custom Level button.

8. In the list of Settings, under Miscellaneous, set the Access data sources across domains option to Enable.

9. Click OK to close the Security Settings dialog box.

10. Click OK to close the Internet Options dialog box.

For other ways to allow blocked features, see the Microsoft Knowledge Base article "You Cannot Run Executable Files or Program Add-Ins That Are Downloaded by Using Internet Explorer or by Using Outlook Express on a Windows XP Service Pack 2-Based Computer," at `http://support.microsoft.com/?id=843022`.

10.5. Using AutoRepublish: The Don't Show This Message Again Option

Problem

When you save a previously published Excel file in which the AutoRepublish feature has been enabled, you see a message that says, "This workbook contains items that are automatically republished to Web pages each time the workbook is saved." There are two options: Disable the AutoRepublish feature while this workbook is open, and Enable the AutoRepublish feature.

At the bottom of the message is the Do not show this message again check box. You checked the box and no longer see the message, but you'd like to reenable it so you see the message when saving the file.

Solution

When you check the Do not show this message again box, an entry is created in the Windows Registry. You can change the entry to reenable the message.

■**Caution** If you decide to modify the Microsoft Windows Registry, as described next, make a backup copy of the Registry first, and be sure that you know how to restore the Registry if there's a problem. There's information on using the Windows Registry in the Microsoft Knowledge Base article "Description of the Microsoft Windows Registry," at `http://support.microsoft.com/kb/256986/`.

---

1. Close Excel.

2. On the Windows Taskbar, click the Start button, and then choose Run.

3. In the Open box, type **regedit**, and click OK.

4. Expand HKEY_CURRENT_USER | Software | Microsoft | Office | 11.0 | Excel.

5. Click Options, and in the right pane, select the DisableAutoRepublishWarning option (see Figure 10-6).

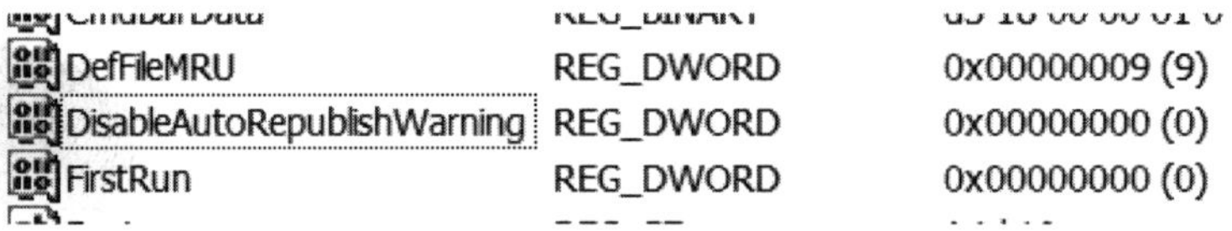

CmdbarData	REG_BINARY	d5 10 00 00 01 0
DefFileMRU	REG_DWORD	0x00000009 (9)
DisableAutoRepublishWarning	REG_DWORD	0x00000000 (0)
FirstRun	REG_DWORD	0x00000000 (0)

Figure 10-6. *The DisableAutoRepublishWarning setting in the Registry Editor*

6. Choose Edit ➤ Modify.

7. In the Value data box, change the 0 to a 1. (Zero sets the DisableAutoRepublishWarning option to Off, and one sets the DisableAutoRepublishWarning option to On.)

8. Click OK to close the Edit DWORD Value dialog box.

9. Choose File ➤ Exit to close the Registry Editor.

10. Start Excel, and the AutoRepublish message will appear when you save a previously published file.

CHAPTER 11

Printing a Pivot Table

One of the strengths of pivot tables is the ability to change the layout and analyze data from different perspectives. Sometimes, though, you want a static picture from the pivot table and need to print the data. For the most part, pivot tables print the same as other data on a worksheet, but there are a few special settings that you can apply to a pivot table.

Some printing issues, such as printing a copy of the pivot table for each item in the page field, can be solved by programming, and examples are given in Chapter 13.

11.1. Repeating Pivot Table Headings

Problem

Your pivot table spans several printed pages, and the page, row and column headings only print on the first page. You want the headings on every page so readers can understand the report.

Solution

You can set an option for the pivot table to make the page, row, and column headings appear on every sheet when you print the pivot table.

Before you turn on this option, clear any entries for row and column titles on the worksheet:

1. On the Excel Worksheet menu, choose File ➤ Page Setup.

2. On the Sheet tab, under Print titles, clear the Rows to repeat at top and Columns to repeat at left boxes.

3. Click OK to close the Page Setup dialog box.

■Note If either of these boxes contains an entry, the Set print titles option won't be applied.

---

4. Right-click a cell in the pivot table, and choose Table Options.

5. Add a checkmark to Set print titles.

■Note Only one pivot table per worksheet can have the Set print titles option selected.

---

6. Click OK to close the PivotTable Options dialog box.

■Tip If you clear the Print titles settings in the Page Setup dialog box after turning on the Set print titles option, you'll have to turn the Set print titles option off, then turn it back on, for it to take effect.

How It Works

When the Set print titles option is selected, the page, row, and column headings for the pivot table print on every page. If there are multiple pivot tables on the worksheet, or other data, the pivot table headings will also print with those.

For example, you may have a pivot table in cells A1:F300, and a summary in cells L1:M4, with the print area set for cells L1:M4. If Set print titles is selected for the pivot table, the page and row fields headings that are in rows 1:4 will print at the top left of the page, even though they're not included in the print area (see Figure 11-1).

	A	B	L	M
1			**Sales Summary**	
2	SalesMgr	(All)	Bars	4,048,443
3	Status	(All)	Cookies	5,353,078
4	Product	(All)	Crackers	10,754,142

Figure 11-1. *The pivot table print titles appear even when the print area is set for L1:M4.*

11.2. Setting the Print Area to Fit the Pivot Table

Problem

Your pivot table frequently changes size, and you have to reset the print area every time you want to print it.

Solution

Don't set a print area on the sheet with the pivot table, and the entire pivot table will print, no matter what its size, although it may span several sheets of paper. To remove an existing print area, on the Excel Worksheet menu choose File ➤ Print Area ➤ Clear Print Area.

If you're setting a print area because there are other items on the sheet that you don't want to print, move those items to another sheet, if possible, so you can print the pivot table separately. If the items must remain on the same sheet as the pivot table, use the following technique to quickly set a print area that encompasses the entire pivot table.

Quickly Setting a Print Area for the Entire Pivot Table

1. Right-click a cell in the pivot table, and choose Select ➤ Entire Table.

2. From the Excel worksheet menu, choose File ➤ Print Area ➤ Set Print Area.

■**Tip** You can add a Set Print Area button to one of your toolbars by using the Tools ➤ Customize command.

11.3. Compacting the Space Required for Row Labels

Problem

There are several row fields in your pivot table, and when you print, the row field labels fill the first page. You'd like to reduce the space required for the labels so it's easier to read the printed report.

Solution

With the pivot table in Outline layout, you can reduce the column width for many of the row fields:

1. Double-click the field button for the outer row field.

2. Click the Layout button to open the PivotTable Field Layout dialog box.

3. Select the Show items in outline form option, and add a checkmark to Display subtotals at top of group.

4. Click OK to close the PivotTable Field Layout dialog box.

5. Click OK to close the PivotTable Field dialog box.

6. Repeat Steps 1–5 for each remaining row field, except the innermost field.

7. At the top of the worksheet, select the columns for all the row fields that you formatted.

8. Adjust the width of the selected columns so they show only a few characters.

9. At the left of the worksheet, select the row that contains the row field buttons.

10. In the Excel worksheet menu, choose Format ➤ Cells.

11. On the Alignment tab, change the Orientation to 90 degrees, and set the Horizontal Text alignment to Center.

12. Click OK to close the Format Cells dialog box.

The pivot table row fields now require much less space, and the labels and data may fit on the same printed page, as shown in Figure 11-2.

| Sum of Qty | | | | | YearNo |
SalesMgr	Customer	Category	Product	Status	2004
Boston					**3,758,085**
	Corner Cabin				1,244,103
		Crackers			662,827
			Cheese		82,676
				Forecast	41,187
				Actual	41,489

Figure 11-2. *The column width is reduced with the pivot table in Outline layout.*

11.4. Printing the Pivot Table for Each Page Item

Problem

You need to give each salesperson a printed copy of the pivot table with their sales results visible.

Solution

You can use the Show Pages feature to create a worksheet for each item in the Salesperson page field:

1. On the PivotTable toolbar, choose PivotTable ➤ Show Pages.

2. If there are multiple page fields, the Show Pages dialog box will appear. Select the Salesperson field, and click the OK button.

3. Select all the worksheets that were created, and print them.

4. After printing, you can delete the sheets that were created by the Show Pages command, or close the workbook without saving the changes.

11.5. Printing Field Items: Starting Each Item on a New Page

Problem

Your pivot table has Customer and Product in the row area, and when you print your pivot table, you want each customer's data to start on a new page.

Solution

You can set the Customer field so each item starts on a new page:

1. Right-click the Customer field button, and choose Field Settings.

2. Click the Layout button, and add a checkmark to Insert page break after each item.

3. Click OK to close the PivotTable Field Layout dialog box, and click OK to close the PivotTable Field dialog box.

Tip When starting each item on a new page, your pivot table may be easier to understand if you set the pivot table print titles, as described in Section 11.1. This repeats the pivot table headings on each page, so they'll be visible with each customer's data.

Notes

Depending on how you've formatted the pivot table, the bottom border may be missing from each customer's subtotal when you use the Insert page break after each item option (see Figure 11-3).

	Rice Wafers	79,455
	Saltines	77,697
	Vanilla Thins	81,254
	Whole Wheat	86,472
Corner Cabin Total		1,244,103

Figure 11-3. *The bottom border is missing when the Insert page break after each item option is used.*

To ensure that the border prints, you can format the subtotal row:

1. Point to the left edge of a subtotal row, and when the pointer changes to a thick black arrow, click to select all the subtotal rows for that field.

2. On the Excel Worksheet menu, choose Format ➤ Cells.

3. On the Border tab, if the bottom border is showing in the preview area, click on it to remove it (see Figure 11-4).

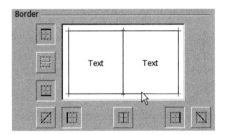

Figure 11-4. *Click the bottom border in the preview area to turn it off.*

4. Then, click the bottom border in the preview area to turn it on.

5. Click OK to close the Format Cells dialog box.

11.6. Printing Field Items: Keeping All Rows for an Item on One Page

Problem

In the Row area of your pivot table, you have the Salesperson and Product fields. You want to keep all the information for each salesperson on one page, so if there isn't room on the current page, their information should start on the next page. You can do this in Microsoft Word if you use the Keep with next setting for a paragraph.

Solution

Unlike Microsoft Word, a pivot table doesn't have a setting to keep items together. You can manually adjust the page breaks in Page Break Preview, or set each item to start on a new page, as described in Section 11.5.

Notes

Using the Insert page break after each item setting won't ensure that all items for a field fit on one page. It only ensures that the next item will start on a new page. For fields with many items, two or more pages may be required.

If many of the fields have a short list of items, your printed report could end up using lots of paper with this setting. You may prefer to turn the setting off and choose View ➤ Page Break Preview to manually adjust the page breaks.

■ **Note** You can't move or delete the page breaks that are created by the Insert page break setting.

11.7. Printing Field Items: Including Labels on Each Page

Problem

Your pivot table has Category, Customer, and Product fields in the row area, and each category's data fills two or three pages. The first page shows the category name, but it doesn't appear on subsequent pages. Customer names are missing too if their data continues on a second page (see Figure 11-5).

Salesperson	(All)	
Sum of Qty		
Category	Customer	Product
		Peanuts
		Potato Chips
		Pretzels

Figure 11-5. *The Category and Customer labels are missing at the top of page two.*

Solution

You can change a pivot table option so the labels appear on each page:

1. Right-click a cell in the pivot table, and choose Table Options.

2. Add a checkmark to Repeat item labels on each printed page.

3. Click OK to close the PivotTable Options dialog box.

■**Note** This setting will have no effect if the table option for Merge Labels is turned on.

Notes

This setting can work in conjunction with the Set Print Titles pivot table option, described in Section 11.1. That setting ensures that the columns and rows that contain the headings appear on each printed page. The Repeat item labels on each printed page pivot table option ensures that labels print at the top of each page if an item runs on to two or more pages. In Figure 11-6, both options are turned on, so headings and labels appear on each page.

Salesperson	(All)	

Sum of Qty		
Category	Customer	Product
Crackers	Giant Grocer	Peanuts
		Potato Chips
		Pretzels

Figure 11-6. *The Category and Customer labels repeat at the top of page two.*

11.8. Using Report Manager: Printing Pivot Table Data

Problem

Because of security settings, you can't distribute a workbook that contains macros. You'd like to make it easy for users to print summary reports from the pivot table data.

Solution

Microsoft provides an Excel add-in, Report Manager, that you can use to create and print reports from worksheets, custom views, and scenarios. The download file and installation instructions are available on the Microsoft website "Excel 2002 Add-in: Report Manager," at www.microsoft.com/downloads/details.aspx?FamilyID=34dacd92-d511-4760-8094-2754d82a4e2f.

■Note Although the web page title specifies Excel 2002, the Report Manager download can be used in Excel 2003.

To create a summary table from the pivot table data, follow these steps:

1. On a blank worksheet, list the items that you want to summarize. In the example shown in Figure 11-7, items from the Status field are listed in B4:B6, and items from the insurance type (InsType) field are listed in C3:D3. A region name is entered in cell B2, and this is the cell that will change as the reports are printed.

	A	B	C	D	E	F	G
1							
2		East					
3			Auto	Prop			
4		Cancel	=GETPIVOTDATA("Policies",InsurPivot!$A$5,				
5		Existing	"Region",$B$2,"Status",$B4,"InsType",C$3)				
6		New					
7							

Figure 11-7. *A GETPIVOTDATA formula extracts data from the pivot table.*

2. In the summary table, use GETPIVOTDATA formulas to extract data from the pivot table. In cell C4, the formula is

```
=GETPIVOTDATA("Policies",InsurPivot!$A$5,"Region",$B$2,
    "Status",$B4,"InsType",C$3)
```

3. Copy the formula down to the last row heading, and across to the last column heading.

4. Add row and column totals, if desired.

To create a scenario from the current summary, do the following:

1. Select cell B2, and on the Excel worksheet menu, choose Tools ➤ Scenarios.

2. Click the Add button, and type **East** as the scenario name. Leave the default values in the other text boxes.

3. Click OK to open the Scenario Values dialog box, and click OK to confirm the values for the changing cells.

4. Click the Add button, and type the next region name, **West**, as the scenario name.

5. Click OK to open the Scenario Values dialog box, type **West** as the value, and click OK.

6. Click the Show button to see the West region summary on the worksheet.

7. Click Close to close the Scenario Manager.

To create a report from the scenarios, follow these steps:

1. On the Excel worksheet menu, choose View ➤ Report Manager.

2. Click the Add button, and type **Region Summaries** in the Report Name box, as shown in Figure 11-8.

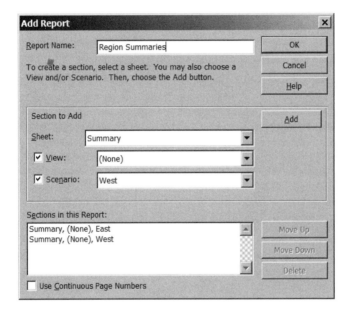

Figure 11-8. *Create new reports in the Add Report dialog box.*

3. From the Sheet dropdown, select the sheet that contains the summary report.

4. From the Scenario dropdown, choose one of the scenarios.

5. Click the Add button to add the scenario to the report.

6. Repeat Steps 3–5 for the remaining scenarios that you want to include in the printed report.

7. Click OK to close the Add Report dialog box, and click Close to close the Report Manager.

To print a report, do the following:

1. On the Excel worksheet menu, choose View ➤ Report Manager.

2. Select a report in the Reports list, and click the Print button.

3. Enter the number of copies you want to print, and click OK.

How It Works

The GETPIVOTDATA formula uses an absolute reference to the region name cell ($B$2), and mixed references to the row and column heading cells, so the formula can be copied across and down:

```
=GETPIVOTDATA("Policies",InsurPivot!$A$5,"Region",$B$2,
  "Status",$B4,"InsType",C$3)
```

For the row headings in cells B4:B6 the column is absolute, $B, and the row is relative. When the formula is copied down or across, the formula will always refer to the data in column B in the current row.

For the column headings in cells C3:D3 the column is relative, C, and the row is absolute, $3. When the formula is copied down or across, the formula will always refer to the data in row 3 in the current column.

When printing the Region Summaries report, the Report Manager shows each selected scenario, prints the summary with that scenario visible, and then shows the next scenario.

CHAPTER 12

■■■

Pivot Charts

When you create a PivotTable report, you can create a PivotChart report at the same time, or you can create a PivotChart report at any time later, based on one of the pivot tables in your workbook. A PivotChart report can't be created on its own; it must be based on a PivotTable report. PivotChart reports are similar to normal Excel charts, but have some differences and limitations, as described in this chapter.

12.1. Stepping Through the Chart Wizard to Create a Pivot Chart

Problem

If you select a cell in the pivot table and click the Chart Wizard button on the Standard toolbar, a default pivot chart on a chart sheet is created. You'd like to step through the Chart Wizard so you can set the options as you create the pivot chart.

Solution

1. Select an empty cell away from the pivot table and any other data on the worksheet.

2. On the Standard toolbar, click the Chart Wizard button.

3. In Step 1 of the Chart Wizard, select a Chart type and Chart sub-type, then click Next.

■**Note** The XY (Scatter), Bubble, and Stock chart types are not available when creating a pivot chart.

---

4. In Step 2 of the Chart Wizard, click in the Data range box, then select any cell in the pivot table. The entire pivot table will be automatically selected, and its address will appear in the Data range box (see Figure 12-1).

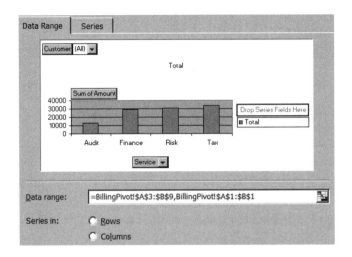

Figure 12-1. *The data range is automatically entered when a pivot table cell is selected.*

5. Continue through the Chart Wizard steps, selecting the options you want, then click Finish to create the pivot chart.

■Note After selecting a pivot table as the data range, you can't return to Step 2 of the Chart Wizard. To use a different data range, create a new chart.

12.2. Creating a Normal Chart from Pivot Table Data

Problem

You want to create a normal chart from the pivot table data, but a pivot chart is automatically created when you select a cell in the pivot table and then click the Chart Wizard button.

Solution

1. Select an empty cell away from the pivot table and any other data on the worksheet.

2. On the Standard toolbar, click the Chart Wizard button.

3. Click Finish to create an empty chart.

4. Select the pivot table data cells and either the series or category axis labels, avoiding the field buttons. For example, in Figure 12-2, the category axis labels (Finance, Risk, and Tax) are selected, along with the data. The Series labels (Jan and Feb) are not selected to avoid selecting the Service field button.

■**Caution** While creating the normal chart, if you select a cell that contains a PivotChart field button, the chart will become a pivot chart.

---

5. Point to the border of the selected range, and drag or copy the selection to the empty chart (see Figure 12-2).

Customer	(All)	▼	
Sum of Amount	DateBill ▼		
Service ▼	Jan	Feb	
Finance	8,048	11,847	
Risk	19,945	5,793	
Tax	11,442	8,615	

Figure 12-2. *Drag the selected range onto the empty chart.*

6. To add the missing labels, right-click the chart, choose Source Data, and select the Series tab.

7. If the Series labels are missing, select a series in the Series list, and click in the Name box. Click the worksheet cell that contains the label for the selected series (see Figure 12-3). Repeat for the remaining series.

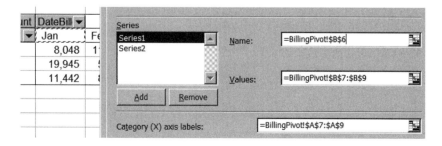

Figure 12-3. *Select the pivot table cell that contains the series label.*

8. If the category axis labels are missing, click in the Category (X) axis labels box. Select the worksheet cells that contain the labels for the category axis.

9. Click OK to close the Source Data dialog box.

12.3. Restoring Lost Series Formatting

Problem

You changed your pivot chart to a line chart type, and made the lines thicker, then changed the colors and markers. When you refresh the pivot chart or change the pivot table, the series formatting in the connected pivot chart is lost.

Solution

Loss of series formatting after a pivot table change or refresh is a known problem with pivot charts. You can create a user-defined custom chart type, and apply that chart type after refreshing the pivot table. Or, record a macro as you apply the series formatting, and then run the macro after you refresh the pivot charts. There are instructions in Chapter 13 for recording and using macros.

Creating a Custom Chart Type

1. Select a chart that's formatted the way you'd like your pivot charts to look.

▩**Note** Any Title text in the custom chart will be included in the format.

---

2. From the Excel Worksheet menu, choose Chart ➤ Chart Type.

3. On the Custom Types tab, select User-defined, then click the Add button.

4. Type a name for the custom chart type, and, if desired, a description.

5. Click OK to close the Add Custom Chart Type dialog box.

6. Click OK to close the Chart Type dialog box.

Applying a Custom Chart Type to a Pivot Chart

1. Right-click the pivot chart that you want to format, and choose Chart Type.

2. Click the Custom Types tab, and select User-defined.

3. Select your Custom chart type, then click OK.

How It Works

The pivot chart formatting is lost because Excel removes the data series when you change the pivot table and then rebuilds the chart, using the default formatting for the selected chart type. It then adds the data series back to the chart. When this occurs, formatting that you previously applied to the data series in the chart is lost.

Notes

If the only change you're making to the formatting is the series color, you can change the color palette, substituting your preferred colors for the default chart colors.

Changing the Default Chart Colors

1. On the Excel Worksheet menu, choose Tools ➤ Options, and select the Color tab.

2. The Chart fills section shows the default area colors for the chart series. Select a Chart fills or Chart lines color, and click the Modify button.

3. On the Standard or Custom tab, select a replacement color.

Tip If selecting a custom color, double-click on the Colors dialog box title bar to maximize it. This will make color selection easier.

---

4. Click OK to close the Colors dialog box.

5. Modify the remaining colors, if desired, then click OK to close the Options dialog box.

Tip On the Color tab of the Options dialog box, you can copy the colors from another open workbook by selecting that workbook in the Copy colors from dropdown list.

12.4. Adjusting Hidden Pie Chart Labels

Problem

The labels on your pivot chart, a pie chart type, are hidden by the field buttons, and you want to make them visible.

Solution

If you create a pivot chart that's a pie chart, some of the labels may be hidden by the pivot buttons. To solve the problem, you can hide the PivotChart field buttons, change the angle of the first slice, or reposition the data labels.

Hiding the PivotChart Field Buttons

1. Select the pivot chart, and on the PivotTable toolbar, choose PivotChart ➤ Hide PivotChart Field Buttons.

Changing the Angle of the First Pie Slice

1. Right-click any slice in the pie chart, and choose Format Data Series.

2. On the Options tab, increase the angle of the first slice until the labels are visible in the preview.

3. Click OK to close the Format Data Series dialog box.

Moving a Single Label

1. Click any one of the data labels to select all of them.

2. Click on the partially hidden data label to select it.

3. Point to the border of the selected data label, and drag it out from under the field button (see Figure 12-4).

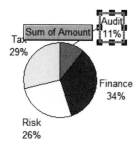

Figure 12-4. *Drag the hidden data label out from under the field button.*

Repositioning All the Data Labels

1. Right-click one of the data labels, and choose Format Data Labels.

2. On the Alignment tab, from the Label Position dropdown list, choose Inside End or Center.

3. Click OK to close the Format Data Labels dialog box.

The data labels will move to inside the pie slices, where they won't be covered by the field button. However, if there are many small slices, the labels may not have enough room in this position.

12.5. Formatting Category Axis Date Labels

Problem

You formatted the dates in your pivot table to show the month and day (mmm-dd). However, the category axis labels in the pivot chart still show the dates as m/d/yyyy, as they appear in the source data. You tried to format the axis, but there's no tab in the Format Axis dialog box for number format.

Solution

The pivot chart number formats are controlled by the field format in the pivot table. If you select the cells that contain dates in the pivot table and format them, the pivot chart date formats won't be affected. Instead, right-click the Date field button in the pivot table and choose Field Settings. Click the Number button, and set the date format there.

12.6. Changing Pivot Chart Layout Affects Pivot Table

Problem

When you change the pivot chart layout, the related pivot table is also changed. You want them to work independently.

Solution

If you rearrange the fields in a pivot chart, the same changes are made to the related pivot table. You can create a second pivot table, based on the first one, and arrange it as you'd like. When you change the pivot chart, only the original pivot table will be affected. You can hide the first pivot table that's connected to the pivot chart and use the second pivot table for displaying or printing.

If you require several charts based on the same pivot table but with different layouts, create multiple pivot tables based on the original pivot table. Create one pivot chart from each of the secondary pivot tables, and rearranging one won't affect the others.

12.7. Resizing and Moving Pivot Chart Elements

Problem

Before printing the pivot chart, you want to make the chart area bigger and move the legend so it's inside the plot area. When you select the chart area, handles appear on its border, but you can't change the size. You can move the legend by right-clicking it, choosing Format Legend, and selecting a position on the Placement tab, but you can't make manual adjustments to its position.

Solution

Some elements in a pivot chart can't be moved or resized, such as the axes' titles, the chart title, the plot area, the legend, and the value axis display unit label. You could create a normal chart from the pivot data, as described in Section 12.2, and you'll have more flexibility in adjusting the chart elements.

12.8. Including Grand Totals in a Pivot Chart

Problem

The grand totals are visible in the pivot table, and you want to include them in the pivot chart.

Solution

The pivot chart is limited to showing the data from the pivot table's data area. Other data, such as grand totals or additional series, such as a target line, can't be added.

You could create a normal chart based on the pivot table, as described in Section 12.2, and include the totals in that.

12.9. Converting a Pivot Chart to a Static Chart

Problem

You want to change a pivot chart to a static chart that isn't connected to the pivot table. That way, you can send the pivot chart to your customer without the underlying detailed data.

Solution

To change a pivot chart to a static chart, you can copy the pivot chart to a different workbook:

1. Select the pivot chart.

2. On the Excel Worksheet menu, choose Edit ➤ Copy.

3. Activate the workbook into which you want to paste the pivot chart.

4. On the Excel Worksheet menu, choose Edit ➤ Paste.

12.10. Using Page Fields: Page Fields with Hidden Items Shows (All)

Problem

In the pivot table, you hid some of the items in the Customer page field by double-clicking the Customer field button and selecting customer names in the Hide Items list. The Customer field in the pivot table shows (Multiple Items), but in the pivot chart, it shows (All).

Solution

You can't change the behavior of the Page field in the pivot chart, but you can add a text box linked to the Customer page field in the pivot table to display the correct title:

1. Select the pivot chart (you don't need to click in the formula bar).

2. Type an equal sign, then select the Customer page field cell in the pivot table.

3. Press the Enter key to complete the formula.

4. To hide the incorrect Customer page field in the pivot chart, fill the text box with white color, and position it over the Customer page field.

CHAPTER 13

Programming a Pivot Table

Although you can create complex pivot tables without programming, some pivot table settings can only be changed by using programming. As a developer, you can use programming to limit the ways that users can manipulate your pivot tables, or to simplify a complex set of tasks. For example, you can provide a button on the worksheet that users can click to format, refresh, and preview a pivot table before printing.

This chapter will address programming issues related to pivot tables and provide code examples for macros that can't be recorded. The chapter begins with a brief introduction to using Excel's macro recorder and the Visual Basic Editor (VBE), where code is stored. Many excellent books are available with instructions and examples for learning how to program in Excel. There is also extensive documentation in the VBE help files and in Excel's help files.

For an introductory tutorial, see "Super-Easy Guide to the Microsoft Office Excel 2003 Object Model" on the Microsoft website:

```
http://msdn.microsoft.com/library/default.asp?url=/library/en-us/
odc_xl2003_ta/html/odc_super.asp
```

13.1. Using Sample Code

Problem

You've obtained sample code from this chapter, and would like to use it in your workbook. You aren't sure where to store the code, or how to run it.

Solution

To use the code examples in this chapter, you can add them to your workbooks. Some code may require modification, as described in Section 13.3, to match names and ranges in your workbooks. You'd then run the code using one of the methods described here.

Storing the Code

Most of the code samples are stored on a regular code module:

1. Download the sample files, and copy the code that you want to use.

2. Open the workbook in which you want to store the code.

3. Hold the Alt key, and press the F11 key to open the Visual Basic Editor.

4. Choose Insert ➤ Module.

5. Where the cursor is flashing, choose Edit ➤ Paste.

Some code is event code, and will run automatically when something specific occurs in the workbook. For example, if you type in a cell and press the Enter key, the worksheet will be changed. This could trigger the Worksheet_Change event. Worksheet event code is stored on a worksheet code module. To add the code to a worksheet, do the following:

1. Download the sample files, and copy the code that you want to use.

2. Select the worksheet in which you want to use the code.

3. Right-click the sheet tab and choose View Code to open the Visual Basic Editor.

4. Where the cursor is flashing, choose Edit ➤ Paste.

Running the Code

Macros can be run by using several methods. For example, you can use a shortcut key, a menu command, or a toolbar button.

Using a Shortcut Key: When recording a macro, you can assign a shortcut key, as described in Section 13.2. To run the macro, press the shortcut key combination.

Using a Menu Command: To run a macro, you can use the command on the Excel Worksheet menu:

1. On Excel's Worksheet menu, choose Tools ➤ Macro ➤ Macros.

2. From the Macros in dropdown list, select the location in which you stored your macro.

3. In the list of macros, select your macro, then click the Run button.

Using a Toolbar Button: To run a macro, you can add a button to a toolbar:

1. On Excel's Worksheet menu, choose Tools ➤ Customize.

2. On the Commands tab, in the Categories list, select Macros.

3. From the Commands list, drag the Custom Button to an existing toolbar.

4. Click the Modify Selection button, and choose Assign Macro.

5. Select a macro from the list, and click OK.

6. Click Close to close the Customize dialog box.

7. To run the macro, click the toolbar button.

13.2. Recording a Macro While Printing a Pivot Table

Problem

You frequently format and print your pivot table, and there are several steps in the process. First, you apply an AutoFormat, then you refresh the data, and finally you preview the report. You would like to create a macro that performs these steps automatically to make the process easier and faster.

Solution

Excel programming is done in the Visual Basic for Applications (VBA) language. When manually changing or creating a pivot table, you can use Excel's macro recorder to create code as you work. Later, you can run the macro as recorded, or adjust the code to make it more flexible, enabling it to run correctly if the worksheet data or layout changes.

The macro recorder doesn't create ideal code. It records what you do with the mouse and keyboard as you manually perform a task, but occasionally, it's unable to record one or more steps, so the resulting code is incomplete. It also includes many recorded steps that may not be necessary in the final code, such as multiple clicks on the scroll bar button to move down the worksheet. However, for simple tasks, or for learning about Excel's object model and programming syntax, it's a useful tool.

Before You Begin Recording

When creating a macro, you can select a range as the first step in the macro and operate on that range, or you can record steps that operate on the currently selected range. In this example, you want the macro to prepare a specific pivot table, so select a cell outside the pivot table, and then select a different worksheet. You'll select the pivot table's worksheet and a cell in the pivot table after you begin recording.

Recording a Macro

1. Choose Tools ➤ Macro ➤ Record New Macro.

2. Type a one-word name for the macro, for example, **Prepare_Pivot**.

3. If you want to run the macro by using a keyboard shortcut, type an upper- or lowercase letter in the Shortcut key box. In this example, uppercase P is used (see Figure 13-1). This setting is optional; there are other ways to run the macro after you've created it.

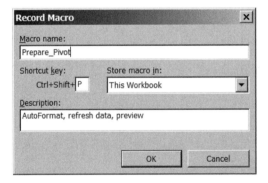

Figure 13-1. *Ctrl+Shift+P is entered as the macro's shortcut key.*

Caution Don't use a shortcut key that's the same as the Excel shortcuts you like to use. For example, Ctrl+c will copy the selection in Excel. If you use Ctrl+c as your macro shortcut, it will overwrite Excel's copy shortcut while the workbook with the macro shortcut is open. However, the shortcut keys are case sensitive; you could hold the Shift key, and use an uppercase C as your shortcut, and it won't overwrite the Copy shortcut.

4. From the Store macro in dropdown, select a location in which to save the macro. In this example, the macro is specific to the active workbook, so you would select This Workbook. If it's a macro that you want to use in many workbooks, you could store it in your Personal Macro Workbook. The third option is to store it in a new workbook.

5. To help you, or other users, understand what the macro does, you can enter a brief message about the macro's purpose in the Description box.

6. Click the OK button to start recording the macro.

7. The Stop Recording toolbar should appear, with two buttons: Stop Recording and Relative Reference (see Figure 13-2).

Figure 13-2. *The Stop Recording toolbar, with the Stop Recording button at the left and the Relative Reference button at the right*

8. Perform the steps that you want to record. In this example, select the pivot table's worksheet, then select a cell at the top left of the pivot table. On the Excel Worksheet menu, choose Format ➤ AutoFormat, select Report 6 AutoFormat, and click OK. Then, on the PivotTable toolbar, click the Refresh Data button. Finally, on the Excel Standard toolbar, click the Print Preview button, and click the Close button.

9. When you've completed the steps that you want to record, click the Stop Recording button on the Stop Recording toolbar.

Viewing the Recorded Code

1. On Excel's Worksheet menu, choose Tools ➤ Macro ➤ Macros.

2. From the Macros in dropdown list, select This Workbook, or the location in which you stored your macro.

3. In the list of macros, select your macro, then click the Edit button (see Figure 13-3).

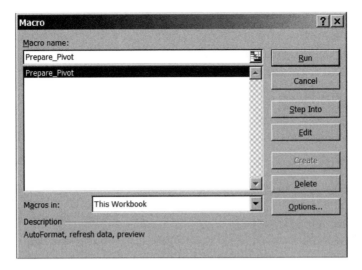

Figure 13-3. *Select your macro in the list, then click the Edit button.*

4. This opens the Visual Basic Editor (VBE), where the recorded code was stored.

5. At the left, you should see the Project Explorer, which lists the open Excel files. Your active workbook is in the list, with its modules and Excel objects listed. The recorded code was stored in a module, which is highlighted in the list (see Figure 13-4).

■**Note** If the Project Explorer is not visible, on the VBE menu choose View ➤ Project Explorer.

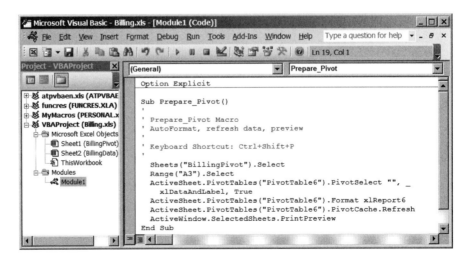

Figure 13-4. *The Visual Basic Editor shows the recorded code.*

6. In the code window at the right, you can see the recorded code. The code is in a procedure, which starts with a line that contains the word Sub, followed by the name you gave the macro and a set of parentheses.

7. Following the Sub line are comment lines that start with a single quote mark. The comments don't affect the code, but can make it easier to understand. Lines that don't start with a single quote mark are the lines of code that control what steps are performed when you run the macro.

Note Although the recorder was on when you closed the Preview window, that step was not recorded.

---

8. In the code window, you can edit the existing code or type new code.

9. To close the VBE and return to Excel, choose File ➤ Close and Return to Microsoft Excel.

Running a Macro

When you're ready to print the pivot table, you can run your macro to perform the preparation steps:

1. On Excel's Worksheet menu, choose Tools ➤ Macro ➤ Macros.

2. From the Macros in dropdown list, select the location in which you stored your macro.

3. In the list of macros, select your macro, then click the Run button (see Figure 13-3).

Changing a Macro Keyboard Shortcut

After creating a macro that runs from a keyboard shortcut, you may want to change the letter used in the shortcut. To do so, follow these steps:

1. On Excel's Worksheet menu, choose Tools ➤ Macro ➤ Macros.

2. From the Macros in dropdown list, select the location in which you stored your macro.

3. In the list of macros, select your macro, then click the Options button (see Figure 13-3).

4. In the Shortcut key box, type a different character.

5. Click OK to close the Macro Options dialog box.

6. Click Cancel to close the Macro dialog box.

13.3. Modifying Recorded Code

Problem

You turned on the macro recorder as you formatted the pivot table, refreshed the data, and previewed the worksheet. The following code was created:

```
Sub Prepare_Pivot()
'
' Prepare_Pivot Macro
' AutoFormat, refresh data, preview
' Keyboard Shortcut: Ctrl+Shift+P
'
    Sheets("BillingPivot").Select
    Range("A3").Select
    ActiveSheet.PivotTables("PivotTable6").PivotSelect "", xlDataAndLabel, True
    ActiveSheet.PivotTables("PivotTable6").Format xlReport6
    ActiveSheet.PivotTables("PivotTable6").PivotCache.Refresh
    ActiveWindow.SelectedSheets.PrintPreview
End Sub
```

You changed the pivot table name, and when you ran the macro, an error message appeared that said, "Run-time error '1004': Unable to get the PivotTables property of the Worksheet class."

Solution

The recorded code includes the name of the pivot table at the time of the recording:

```
ActiveSheet.PivotTables("PivotTable6").PivotCache.Refresh
```

You can replace the recorded name with the new name, and the macro will run correctly.

1. To edit the code, open the VBE, as described in Section 13.2.

2. If the pivot table's new name is BillingPivot, change all occurrences of the recorded name to BillingPivot. For example:

```
ActiveSheet.PivotTables("BillingPivot").PivotCache.Refresh
```

3. Click the Save button, then choose File ➤ Close and Return to Microsoft Excel.

13.4. Showing Top 10 Items over a Set Amount

Problem

Instead of showing data for all salespeople, or the Top 10 salespeople, you want to show only salespeople with sales over $2 million.

Solution

The Top 10 feature lets you show the top or bottom items in a pivot table, based on a specific number of items. You can use programming to count the number of salespeople whose sales total is greater than the specified amount, and show that number of items:

1. On the pivot table worksheet, enter the target value in a cell, away from the pivot table range.

2. With the target value cell selected, click in the Name Box to the left of the formula bar, and type a one-word name for the cell, in this example **MinAmt**. Press the Enter key.

3. Store the following code on a regular code module:

```
Sub TopNCalculate()
    Dim ws As Worksheet
    Dim pt As PivotTable
    Dim pf As PivotField
    Dim df As PivotField
    Dim pi As PivotItem
    Dim rng As Range
    Dim SortOrder As Long
    Dim SortField As String
    Dim Amt As Long
    Dim piCount As Long

    On Error GoTo err_Handler
    Set ws = ActiveSheet
    Set pt = ws.PivotTables(1)
    Set df = pt.PivotFields("Sum of Dollars") 'data field
    Set pf = pt.PivotFields("Salesperson") 'row field
    Amt = ws.Range("MinAmt").Value
    piCount = 0
    Application.ScreenUpdating = False
```

```
        'determine the current sort order and field
        SortOrder = pf.AutoSortOrder
        SortField = pf.AutoSortField
        pf.AutoSort xlManual, SortField 'manual to prevent errors
        pf.AutoShow xlManual, xlTop, 1, df  'manual turns off AutoShow

        For Each pi In pf.PivotItems
            pi.Visible = True
            Set rng = pt.GetPivotData(df.Value, pf.Value, pi.Name)
            If rng.Value >= CLng(Amt) Then
                piCount = piCount + 1  'count items that qualify
            End If
        Next pi

        If piCount > 0 Then
            If piCount = pf.PivotItems.Count Then
                MsgBox "All items exceed entered amount"
            Else
                pf.AutoShow xlAutomatic, xlTop, piCount, df
            End If
        Else
            MsgBox "No items exceed entered amount"
        End If

exit_Handler:
        pf.AutoSort SortOrder, SortField 'restore the AutoSort settings
        Application.ScreenUpdating = True
        Exit Sub

err_Handler:
      MsgBox Err.Number & ": " & Err.Description
      GoTo exit_Handler
End Sub
```

4. Change the value in the MinAmt cell, then run the macro, as described in Section 13.1, to see salespeople who exceeded that amount in sales.

How It Works

The TopNCalculate procedure uses the GetPivotData method, which is similar to the GetPivotData worksheet function, to check the total dollars for each salesperson. If the amount is greater than the amount entered in the MinAmt cell, that Salesperson item is counted. The piCount variable stores the count of items.

In the code, the AutoSort for the Salesperson field is set to xlManual to prevent an error that occurs when trying to show items in a field with AutoSort set to xlAutomatic. At the end of the procedure, the original AutoSort setting is restored.

If no salesperson totals exceed the minimum amount, or if all salesperson totals exceed the minimum amount, the AutoShow feature is turned off, and all items are visible.

13.5. Changing the Summary Function for All Data Fields

Problem

When you add fields to the data area, sometimes they appear as Count of Item instead of Sum of Item. You would like the Sum function to be the default for all data fields.

Solution

You can't change the default settings for the pivot table's data fields; if a field in the source data contains blank cells, or cells with text, it will default to Count; otherwise, it will Sum. After the data fields have been added, you can run a macro to change the summary function. The following macro will change all the data fields in the first pivot table on the active sheet to use the Sum function. Store the code on a regular code module.

```
Sub SumAllDataFields()
  Dim pt As PivotTable
  Dim pf As PivotField
  Dim ws As Worksheet

  Set ws = ActiveSheet
  Set pt = ws.PivotTables(1)
  Application.ScreenUpdating = False

    pt.ManualUpdate = True
    For Each pf In pt.DataFields
      pf.Function = xlSum
    Next pf
    pt.ManualUpdate = False

  Application.ScreenUpdating = True
End Sub
```

To run the code, use a method described in Section 13.1.

How It Works

The SumAllDataFields procedure changes the Function property for each data field, setting it to xlSum. Because the ws variable is set to the ActiveSheet instead of a specific worksheet, you can run the code on any worksheet that contains a pivot table.

13.6. Hiding Rows with a Zero Total for Calculated Items

Problem

When you add calculated items to your pivot table, many rows with a zero total appear in the table, and you want to hide these zero rows.

Solution

You can use programming to quickly hide the rows with a zero total. The following code may hide the first row of an item, including the item label. It works best when the pivot table is in outline form, with the Display subtotals at top of group option turned on.

■**Caution** This code hides worksheet rows, and should not be used if the worksheet contains other information that should remain visible.

---

1. To apply the outline form setting, right-click the outermost row field button, and choose Field Settings.

2. Click the Layout button.

3. Select Show items in outline form, and add a checkmark to Display subtotals at top of group.

4. Click OK to close the PivotTable Field Layout dialog box.

5. Click OK to close the PivotTable Field dialog box.

6. Store the following code on a regular code module:

```
Sub HideZeroRows()
    Dim pt As PivotTable
    Dim DataRow As Range
    Dim ZeroCount As Long
    Dim BlankCount As Long
```

```
      Set pt = ActiveSheet.PivotTables(1)

      Application.ScreenUpdating = False
      For Each DataRow In pt.DataBodyRange.Rows
        ZeroCount = Application.WorksheetFunction.CountIf(DataRow, 0)
        BlankCount = Application.WorksheetFunction.CountBlank(DataRow)
        If ZeroCount + BlankCount = DataRow.Cells.Count Then
          DataRow.EntireRow.Hidden = True
        Else
          DataRow.EntireRow.Hidden = False
        End If
      Next DataRow
      Application.ScreenUpdating = True
    End Sub
```

To run the code, use a method described in Section 13.1. The code refers to ActiveSheet, so you can run the code on any sheet that contains a pivot table.

How It Works

The HideZeroRows procedure checks each row in the pivot table's DataBodyRange, which is the range of cells that contain the data and totals. It uses two worksheet functions: CountIf, to count the cells that contain a zero, and CountBlank, to count the cells that are blank in each row. If the total of blanks and zeros is equal to the number of cells in the row's data range, that worksheet row is hidden; otherwise, the row is made visible.

Notes

You can use another macro to unhide the rows when you want to see them all again:

```
Sub UnhideAllRows()
  Dim DataRow As Range
  Dim pt As PivotTable
  Set pt = ActiveSheet.PivotTables(1)

  Application.ScreenUpdating = False
  For Each DataRow In pt.DataBodyRange.Rows
    DataRow.EntireRow.Hidden = False
  Next DataRow
  Application.ScreenUpdating = True

End Sub
```

13.7. Hiding All Pivot Field Subtotals

Problem

When you add more fields to the row area, some of the fields show subtotals. You want to stop the subtotals from appearing.

Solution

There's no manual setting you can change to stop subtotals from appearing for outer row and column fields, but you can turn the subtotals off programmatically. The following code turns off subtotals for all fields in the first pivot table on the active sheet. Store the code on a regular code module:

```
Sub HideAllPTSubtotals()
  Dim pt As PivotTable
  Dim pf As PivotField

  On Error Resume Next

  Set pt = ActiveSheet.PivotTables(1)

  Application.ScreenUpdating = False
  pt.ManualUpdate = True
  For Each pf In pt.PivotFields
    pf.Subtotals(1) = True
    pf.Subtotals(1) = False
  Next pf
  pt.ManualUpdate = False

  Application.ScreenUpdating = True
End Sub
```

To run the code, use a method described in Section 13.1. The code refers to ActiveSheet, so you can run the code on any sheet that contains a pivot table.

How It Works

The HideAllPTSubtotals code uses a For Each...Next loop to set the subtotal for each pivot field in the pivot table, even the fields that are not visible in the pivot table. First, it sets the pivot field's Subtotals property index to 1, which is the Automatic subtotal setting. This setting turns off any other subtotals that may exist for the pivot table. Then, the automatic subtotals are turned off by changing its setting to False.

■Tip Instead of .PivotFields, you can use pt.RowFields, pt.ColumnFields, or pt.VisibleFields.

The On Error Resume Next line prevents the code from displaying an error message if it can't change the subtotal setting for any pivot field. Instead, it moves on to the next line of code.

To turn on all the subtotals, you could create and run a similar macro, omitting the line that sets the subtotals to False.

13.8. Naming and Formatting the Drill to Details Sheet

Problem

When a user double-clicks a data cell in the pivot table, the underlying records are exported to a new sheet. You'd like to name and format the sheet when it's created by the Drill to Details feature.

Solution

You can use an event procedure that runs when a sheet is added to the workbook to name and format the new sheet.

1. In the VBE, choose Insert ➤ Module.

2. At the top of the module, where the cursor is flashing, type the following line of code to create a public variable. This variable can be used by other procedures in the workbook.

   ```
   Public SheetType As String
   ```

3. In Excel, right-click the pivot table's worksheet tab and choose View Code. Add the following code to the worksheet module:

   ```
   Private Sub Worksheet_BeforeDoubleClick(ByVal Target As Range, _
       Cancel As Boolean)
     Dim pt As PivotTable
   ```

```
    If Me.PivotTables.Count = 0 Then Exit Sub
    For Each pt In Me.PivotTables
      If Not Intersect(Target, pt.DataBodyRange) Is Nothing Then
        SheetType = "Drill"
        Exit For
      End If
    Next pt
End Sub
```

4. In the VBE, in the Project Explorer, double-click the ThisWorkbook object for your workbook. Add the following code to its module, as shown in Figure 13-5:

```
Private Sub Workbook_NewSheet(ByVal Sh As Object)
  On Error GoTo err_Handler
  Select Case SheetType
    Case "Drill"  'Drill to Details
      Sh.Range("A1").CurrentRegion.AutoFormat _
          Format:=xlRangeAutoFormatClassic1
      Sh.Name = Left("XDrill_" & Sh.Name, 31)
    Case Else
      'do nothing
  End Select
  SheetType = ""
err_Handler:
  Exit Sub
End Sub
```

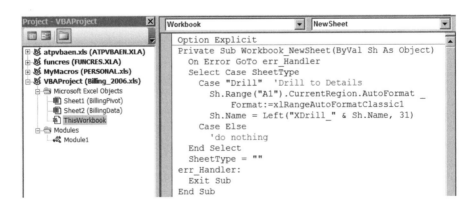

Figure 13-5. *Add code to the ThisWorkbook module.*

To run the event code, double-click a data cell in the pivot table.

How It Works

When any cell on the pivot table's sheet is double-clicked, the BeforeDoubleClick event is triggered. If there are no pivot tables on the worksheet, or the double-clicked cell is not in the DataBodyRange of a pivot table, the procedure is exited. Otherwise, the public variable, SheetType, is set to a value of Drill. If the double-click creates a new sheet, the workbook's NewSheet event code runs. If SheetType is set to Drill, the sheet is given a name that starts with XDrill, and the data on the new sheet is formatted with the Classic 1 AutoFormat.

In the code, sheet names are set to start with XDrill_, so they're easy to identify, and can be deleted automatically when the workbook closes. See Section 13.9 for sample code to delete the worksheets.

13.9. Automatically Deleting Worksheets When Closing a Workbook

Problem

On the PivotTable toolbar, you can choose PivotTable ➤ Show Pages to create a worksheet with a copy of the pivot table for each item in the page field. This command is useful for printing, but adds several pages to the workbook. You'd like these sheets to be automatically deleted when the workbook is closed to prevent the buildup of sheets.

Solution

You can use an event procedure that runs when a sheet is added to the workbook to rename the new sheets so they're easy to identify and delete when the workbook closes.

1. In the ThisWorkbook module, add the following two procedures:

```
Private Sub Workbook_NewSheet(ByVal Sh As Object)
  If TypeName(Sh)="Worksheet" Then
    If Sh.PivotTables.Count > 0 Then
      Sh.Name = Left("XShow_" & Sh.Name, 31)
    End If
  End If
End Sub
'
Private Sub Workbook_BeforeClose(Cancel As Boolean)
  Dim ws As Worksheet
  Dim Resp As Long
  Dim ShowCount As Long
```

```
    ShowCount = 0
    For Each ws In ThisWorkbook.Worksheets
      If UCase(Left(ws.Name, 5)) = "XSHOW" Then
        ShowCount = ShowCount + 1
      End If
    Next ws

    If ShowCount > 0 Then
      Resp = MsgBox("Delete Show Pages sheets?", _
               vbYesNo, "Delete Sheets?")
      If Resp = vbYes Then
        Application.DisplayAlerts = False
        For Each ws In ThisWorkbook.Worksheets
          If UCase(Left(ws.Name, 5)) = "XSHOW" Then
            ws.Delete
          End If
        Next ws
      End If
    End If
End Sub
```

2. To run the event code, select a cell in the pivot table and choose PivotTable ➤ Show Pages on the PivotTable toolbar.

How It Works

If a new sheet is created, the workbook's NewSheet event is triggered. If the new sheet contains a pivot table, it's assumed to be generated by the Show Pages command, and is renamed by the NewSheet code, with XShow_ at the start of the name. When the workbook closes, the workbook's BeforeClose event is triggered. The event code asks the user if Show Pages sheets should be deleted. If the user clicks the Yes button, the sheets are deleted, and the workbook is saved without the sheets.

■Note To use this code to delete the Drill to Detail sheets created with the sample code in Section 13.8, change the code to check for XDRILL instead of XSHOW.

13.10. Changing the Page Field Selection in Related Tables

Problem

In your workbook, two pivot tables are based on the same Excel list. You want to change the Salesperson page field items in both pivot tables at the same time, instead of going to each sheet and changing them individually.

Solution

You can use an event procedure to change the second pivot table's page field when the Salesperson page field is changed in the first pivot table.

1. Enter the following module level variable in the declarations area at the top of the first pivot table sheet's module:

```
Dim mstrPage As Variant
```

2. Below the declarations area, add the following code, changing the sheet name to your second pivot table's sheet name. Also, change the page field name from Salesperson to the name of your page field:

```
Private Sub Worksheet_PivotTableUpdate(ByVal Target As PivotTable)
   Dim wsOther As Worksheet
   Dim pt As PivotTable
   Dim strPage As String

   On Error GoTo err_Handler

   Set wsOther = Worksheets("PivotOther") 'second PT sheet name
   strPage = "Salesperson"                'page field name

   Application.EnableEvents = False

   If UCase(Target.PivotFields(strPage).CurrentPage) _
      <> UCase(mstrPage) Then
     mstrPage = Target.PivotFields(strPage).CurrentPage
     For Each pt In wsOther.PivotTables
       pt.PageFields(strPage).CurrentPage = mstrPage
     Next pt
   End If
```

```
err_Handler:
  Application.EnableEvents = True
End Sub
```

To run the event code, change the selection in the first pivot table's page field.

How It Works

A variable within a procedure is stored only as long as the procedure that declared it is running. A module level variable is used in this example, because it can store the current page field selection while the workbook is open. When the pivot table is updated, the variable named mstrPage is compared to the current page in the Salesperson page field. If they're different, the new page field value is stored in the variable, and the page fields in related pivot tables are changed to match the page field in the main pivot table.

13.11. Clearing Old Items from Field Dropdown Lists

Problem

You deleted some records from the Excel list on which your pivot table is based, but the old items remain in the pivot field dropdown lists, and you'd like to remove them.

Solution

For non-OLAP based pivot tables, you can programmatically change the pivot cache's MissingItemsLimit property to prevent missing items from appearing. The following code sets a missing items limit of zero for each pivot cache in the active workbook. Store the procedure in a regular code module.

▪Note If the MissingItemsLimit property is used in code for an OLAP-based pivot table, a runtime error can occur.

```
Sub SetMissingItemsLimit()
  Dim pc As PivotCache

    For Each pc In ActiveWorkbook.PivotCaches
      pc.MissingItemsLimit = xlMissingItemsNone
      pc.Refresh
    Next pc
End Sub
```

To run the code, use a method described in Section 13.1. The code refers to ActiveWork-book, so you can run the code on any workbook that contains a pivot table.

How It Works

Setting the MissingItemsLimit property to 0 (xlMissingItemsNone) prevents items with no data in the pivot cache from appearing in the pivot field dropdown lists. The pivot cache is refreshed to clear any existing old items.

13.12. Hiding All Items in a Pivot Field

Problem

You can manually check the Show All box to show or hide all items in a pivot table field. When you record this step, the code shows a list of all the items in the pivot field, instead of using a ShowAll command. If you add new items to the field and run the macro, the new items aren't hidden.

Solution

There's no HideAll or ShowAll command available for programming a pivot field. In some cases, the quickest way to show all items is to remove the field from the pivot table, refresh the pivot table, then add the field back to the pivot table. You can also loop through the items in the field, and show or hide them. For example, the following code hides all items, except the last item, in all row fields, in all tables on the active sheet. Store the code on a regular module.

```
Sub HideVisiblePivotItems()
    Dim pt As PivotTable
    Dim pf As PivotField
    Dim pi As PivotItem
    Dim SortOrder As Long
    Dim SortField As String
    Dim ws As Worksheet

    On Error Resume Next

    Set ws = ActiveSheet

    Application.ScreenUpdating = False
    Application.DisplayAlerts = False
```

```
  For Each pt In ws.PivotTables
    pt.ManualUpdate = True
    For Each pf In pt.RowFields
      SortOrder = pf.AutoSortOrder
      SortField = pf.AutoSortField
      pf.AutoSort SortOrder, SortField
      For Each pi In pf.PivotItems
        pi.Visible = False
      Next pi
      pf.AutoSort SortOrder, SortField
    Next pf
  Next pt

exit_Handler:
  Application.ScreenUpdating = True
  Exit Sub
err_Handler:
  MsgBox Err.Number & ": " & Err.Description
  GoTo exit_Handler
End Sub
```

To run the code, use a method described in Section 13.1. The code refers to ActiveSheet, so you can run the code on any sheet that contains a pivot table.

How It Works

The HideVisiblePivotItems code uses For Each...Next loops to set the Visible property for all pivot items in all row fields.

■Tip To hide column fields, change pt.RowFields to pt.ColumnFields.

The On Error Resume Next line prevents the code from displaying an error message if it can't change the Visible property for a pivot item. Instead, it moves to the next line of code.

13.13. Changing Content in the Data Area

Problem

You'd like to change some of the content in the data area of the pivot table, but when you try, you see the error message "Cannot change this part of a PivotTable report."

Solution

If you change a PivotTable setting programmatically, you can make temporary changes to the PivotTable data. Store the code in a regular code module.

```
Sub ChangePTData()
  Dim pt As PivotTable

  Set pt = ActiveSheet.PivotTables(1)
  pt.EnableDataValueEditing = True
End Sub
```

■**Note** When the pivot table is refreshed, the manually entered data will be overwritten.

To run the code, use a method described in Section 13.1. The code refers to ActiveSheet, so you can run the code on any sheet that contains a pivot table.

How It Works

The EnableDataValueEditing property can only be set programmatically, and it allows temporary changes to the pivot table data area cells.

13.14. Identifying a Pivot Table's Pivot Cache

Problem

Several pivot tables in your workbook are based on the same Excel list, and you want to identify which pivot cache each pivot table uses.

Solution

To determine which pivot cache a pivot table uses, you can run the following code to test the pivot table's CacheIndex property and view the result in a message box. Store the code on a regular code module.

```
Sub ViewCacheIndex()
  Dim pcIndex As Long
  On Error GoTo err_Handler
  pcIndex = ActiveCell.PivotTable.CacheIndex
```

```
  MsgBox "PivotCache: " & pcIndex
  Exit Sub
err_Handler:
  MsgBox "Active cell is not in a pivot table"
End Sub
```

Select a cell in a pivot table, then run the code, using a method described in Section 13.1. A message box will display the CacheIndex property for the active cell's pivot table. If the active cell is not in a pivot table, an error message is displayed.

How It Works

When pivot caches are created, they are added to the workbook's PivotCaches collection and given an index number. This number is displayed in the macro's message box.

Another option is to create a user-defined function (UDF) that returns the PivotCache index number for a range so you can see the number on a worksheet. To create a UDF, enter the following code on a regular code module:

```
Function PTCacheIndex(rng As Range)
  PTCacheIndex = rng.PivotTable.PivotCache.Index
End Function
```

To use the UDF, follow these steps:

1. On a worksheet, select the cell in which you want to see the PivotCache index number.

2. From the Excel Worksheet menu, choose Insert ➤ Function.

3. In the Insert Function dialog box, from the select a category dropdown, select User Defined.

4. In the list of functions, select PTCacheIndex, and click OK.

5. In the Function Arguments dialog box, click in the Rng box.

6. Select a cell in the pivot table for which you want to see the pivot cache index number. In this example, the pivot table starts in cell A3 (see Figure 13-6).

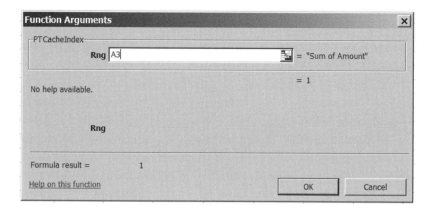

Figure 13-6. *Select a cell in the pivot table as the Rng argument in the UDF.*

7. Click OK to close the Function Arguments dialog box and to see the function results.

13.15. Changing a Pivot Table's Pivot Cache

Problem

You used the code from the previous problem to identify the pivot cache used by each pivot table in your workbook. You want to change the pivot cache of one pivot table so it uses the same cache as another pivot table.

Solution

To change the pivot cache, you can set the pivot table's CacheIndex property. The following code will set the pivot table for the active cell to use pivot cache number 2. Store the code on a regular code module.

```
Sub SetCacheIndex()
  On Error GoTo err_Handler
  ActiveCell.PivotTable.CacheIndex = 2
  Exit Sub
err_Handler:
  MsgBox "Cache index could not be changed"
End Sub
```

To run the code, use a method described in Section 13.1. The code refers to ActiveCell, so you can run the code on any sheet that contains a pivot table.

How It Works

The code sets the CacheIndex property for the active cell's pivot table to 2. If a pivot table cell is not selected, an error message is displayed.

Notes

If you have created several pivot tables in a workbook, based on the same source data, you may find it more efficient to use the same pivot cache for all the pivot tables. This uses less memory than having a separate pivot cache for each pivot table. The following code will change the pivot cache for each pivot table in the workbook, so all pivot tables use the pivot cache of the active cell's pivot table. Store the code in a regular code module.

```
Sub ChangeAllPivotCaches()
  Dim pt As PivotTable
  Dim ws As Worksheet
  On Error GoTo err_Handler

  For Each ws In ActiveWorkbook.Worksheets
    For Each pt In ws.PivotTables
      pt.CacheIndex = ActiveCell.PivotTable.CacheIndex
    Next pt
  Next ws
  Exit Sub
err_Handler:
  MsgBox "Cache index could not be changed"
End Sub
```

Select a cell in the pivot table that uses the pivot cache you want all pivot tables to use. Then run the code, using a method from Section 13.1. Because the code refers to ActiveCell instead of a specific range, you can run the code on any worksheet that contains a pivot table.

13.16. Identifying the Query Used as the Data Source

Problem

Someone else built the pivot table from a Microsoft Access query, and you need to know which query they used as the source and find the path and name of the Access file.

Solution

The following code enters the connection string for the active cell's pivot table on a work-sheet named Connection, where it can be edited. Store the code on a regular code module.

```
Sub ListConnection()
  Dim pt As PivotTable
  Dim ws As Worksheet
  On Error GoTo err_Handler

  Set pt = ActiveCell.PivotTable
  Set ws = Worksheets("Connection")

  ws.Cells.ClearContents
  ws.Cells(2, 1).Value = pt.PivotCache.Connection
  ws.Cells(3, 1).Value = pt.PivotCache.CommandText
  Exit Sub

err_Handler:
  MsgBox "Connection could not be shown"
End Sub
```

Then, follow these steps:

1. Before running the code, create a worksheet named Connection.

2. Select a cell in the pivot table for which you want to view the connection string, and run the ListConnection macro, using a method described in Section 13.1.

How It Works

The ListConnection macro clears the cells on the Connection worksheet, and enters the connection string for the active cell's pivot table in cell A2. In cell A3, it enters the command text string, that shows the query name and the fields that were used.

Tip To view the strings in the cells, you can widen column A, and make rows 2 and 3 taller. Format cells A2 and A3 with Wrap Text (Format ➤ Cells, Alignment tab).

If the database on which the pivot table is based has been moved, you may need to connect the pivot table to the database in its new location. You can modify the connection string to enter the new location for the database. The edited connection string can be used to programmatically update the pivot cache connection.

1. Add the following code to a regular code module:

```
Sub UpdateConnection()
    Dim pt As PivotTable
    Dim ws As Worksheet
    On Error Resume Next

    Set ws = Worksheets("Connection")
    Set pt = ActiveCell.PivotTable

    pt.PivotCache.Connection = ws.Cells(2, 1).Value
    pt.RefreshTable

End Sub
```

2. Run the ListConnection macro to enter the current connection string on the Connection worksheet.

3. On the Connection worksheet, edit the connection string in cell A2 to include the new path for the database.

4. Select a cell in the pivot table for which you want to change the connection.

5. Run the UpdateConnection macro to update the connection string.

13.17. Refreshing a Pivot Table on a Protected Sheet

Problem

You want to refresh a pivot table that's on a protected worksheet, but the Refresh Data button on the PivotTable toolbar is disabled.

Solution

You can record a macro, modify it slightly, and then run that macro when you need to refresh the pivot table.

1. Record a macro as you unprotect the sheet, refresh the pivot table, then protect the worksheet.

2. View the recorded code in the VBE. For example, your code may look similar to the following:

```
Sub RefreshPivot()
  ActiveSheet.Unprotect
  Range("B1").Select
  ActiveSheet.PivotTables("BillingPivot").PivotCache.Refresh
  ActiveSheet.Protect DrawingObjects:=True, _
    Contents:=True, Scenarios:=True
End Sub
```

3. In the recorded code, you can add a password to the Unprotect and Protect lines. For example, if your password is pwd, the revised code would be as follows:

```
Sub RefreshPivot()
  ActiveSheet.Unprotect Password:="pwd"
  Range("B1").Select
  ActiveSheet.PivotTables("BillingPivot").PivotCache.Refresh
  ActiveSheet.Protect Password:="pwd", _
    DrawingObjects:=True, Contents:=True, Scenarios:=True
End Sub
```

4. Run the macro using one of the methods shown in Section 13.1.

How It Works

The RefreshPivot macro stores your password, and uses it when unprotecting and protecting the worksheet. While the worksheet is unprotected, it refreshes the pivot table.

Notes

If you add your password to the macro, it will be visible to anyone who can open your workbook project in the VBE. For information on protecting your code, see the article "Locking Your Solution's VBA Project," at

```
http://msdn.microsoft.com/library/default.asp?url=/library/en-us/odeopg/html/
deovrlockingyoursolutionsvbaproject.asp
```

13.18. Refreshing Automatically When Source Data Changes

Problem

You want the pivot table to automatically refresh when changes are made in the Excel list on which the pivot table is based.

Solution

You can use an event procedure to automatically update the pivot table if the source data changes:

1. Add the following code to the Excel list's worksheet module:

```
Private Sub Worksheet_Change(ByVal Target As Range)
    Worksheets("Pivot").PivotTables(1).PivotCache.Refresh
End Sub
```

2. Modify the code to include the worksheet name for your pivot table.

3. To run the event code, make a change to the data in the Excel list.

How It Works

When there is a change on the Excel list's worksheet, that sheet's Change event is triggered. In the Event code, the specified pivot table's pivot cache is refreshed.

13.19. Preventing Selection of (All) in a Page Field

Problem

You want to prevent users from choosing (All) in a page field.

Solution

You can't remove the (All) option from the page field list, but you can use programming to prevent users from selecting that option. The following code, stored on the pivot table sheet's module, will select the first visible item in the list if (All) is selected, and displays a message warning that the (All) option is not available:

```
Private Sub Worksheet_PivotTableUpdate(ByVal Target As PivotTable)
  Dim pf As PivotField
  Dim i As Long

  Application.EnableEvents = False
  Application.ScreenUpdating = False

  For Each pf In Target.PageFields
    If pf.CurrentPage = "(All)" Then
      i = 1
      For i = 1 To pf.PivotItems.Count + 1
        On Error Resume Next
        pf.CurrentPage = pf.PivotItems(i).Name
        If Err.Number = 0 Then
          Exit For
        End If
      Next i
      MsgBox "The (All) option is not available"
    End If
  Next pf

err_Handler:
  Application.EnableEvents = True
  Application.ScreenUpdating = True
End Sub
```

To run the code, select an item from a page field dropdown list.

How It Works

When an item is selected from a page field's dropdown list, the PivotTableUpdate event is triggered. If the (All) item was selected, the code loops through the page field items, and displays the first available item.

13.20. Disabling Pivot Field Dropdowns

Problem

You want to prevent users from selecting a different item in the field dropdown lists.

Solution

You can use programming to disable many pivot table features. For example, the following macro will disable selection in each field in the first pivot table of the active sheet. The dropdown arrows disappear, and users can't change the displayed items. Store the code in a regular code module.

Note Instead of PivotFields, you can use VisibleFields, RowFields, ColumnFields, or PageFields.

```
Sub DisableSelection()
  Dim pt As PivotTable
  Dim pf As PivotField

  Set pt = ActiveSheet.PivotTables(1)

  For Each pf In pt.PivotFields
    pf.EnableItemSelection = False
  Next pf
End Sub
```

To run the code, use a method described in Section 13.1. The code refers to ActiveSheet, so you can run the code on any sheet that contains a pivot table.

How It Works

The code sets the EnableItemSelection property to False for each field in the pivot table, even if they aren't visible in the layout. To reenable selection, create and run a similar macro that sets the EnableItemSelection property to True.

13.21. Preventing Layout Changes in a Pivot Table

Problem

You want to prevent users from rearranging the pivot table layout.

Solution

The Pivot Table has DragTo settings that you can change programmatically. For example, the following macro prevents dragging fields to any pivot table area or off the pivot table. Store the code in a regular code module.

■**Caution** After using this code, Excel may hang if you attempt to drag the Data button.

```
Sub RestrictPTDrag()
  Dim pt As PivotTable
  Dim pf As PivotField

  Set pt = ActiveSheet.PivotTables(1)

  For Each pf In pt.PivotFields
    With pf
      If .Name <> "Data" Then
        .DragToPage = False
        .DragToRow = False
        .DragToColumn = False
        .DragToData = False
        .DragToHide = False
      End If
    End With
  Next pf
End Sub
```

To run the code, use a method described in Section 13.1. The code refers to ActiveSheet, so you can run the code on any sheet that contains a pivot table.

How It Works

The code stops users from dragging the pivot table fields to a different location. To allow dragging again, create and run a similar macro that sets the DragTo properties to True.

13.22. Preventing Changes to the Pivot Table

Problem

You want to prevent users from making changes to the pivot table, but you can't use worksheet protection, because users need unrestricted access to other items on the worksheet.

Solution

In addition to the security features discussed in the previous sections, you can programmatically control access to the following features:

- Field List

- Field Settings

- Refresh

- Wizard

- Drill to Details

The following macro turns off each of these features. Store the macro on a regular code module.

```
Sub RestrictPTChanges()
  Dim pt As PivotTable
  Dim pf As PivotField

  Set pt = ActiveSheet.PivotTables(1)

  With pt
    .EnableWizard = False
    .EnableDrilldown = False
    .EnableFieldList = False
    .EnableFieldDialog = False
    .PivotCache.EnableRefresh = False
  End With
End Sub
```

To run the code, use a method described in Section 13.1. The code refers to ActiveSheet, so you can run the code on any sheet that contains a pivot table.

How It Works

The RestrictPTChanges macro turns off many features in the first pivot table in the active sheet. To allow use of the features, run another macro that changes the settings to True.

13.23. Viewing Information on Pivot Caches

Problem

Your workbook contains several pivot tables, and you aren't sure how many pivot caches there are, or how much memory is being used. You'd like a summary of the pivot cache information so you can make changes, if necessary, to help the workbook's performance.

Solution

The following procedure creates a new worksheet, with a list of pivot caches in the active workbook and details on each pivot cache. If multiple pivot caches use the same source data, you can set the pivot tables to use one of these caches, and the duplicate will be eliminated. Store the code in a regular code module.

```
Sub ListPivotCacheInfo()
  Dim pc As PivotCache
  Dim wb As Workbook
  Dim ws As Worksheet
  Dim CountRow As Long

  CountRow = 1
  Set wb = ActiveWorkbook

  On Error Resume Next
  Application.DisplayAlerts = False
  Worksheets("Cache_Info").Delete
  Application.DisplayAlerts = True
  On Error GoTo 0

  Set ws = Worksheets.Add
  ws.Name = "Cache_Info"

  With ws
    .Cells(CountRow, 1).Value = "Cache Index"
    .Cells(CountRow, 2).Value = "Command Text"
    .Cells(CountRow, 3).Value = "Command Type"
    .Cells(CountRow, 4).Value = "Connection"
    .Cells(CountRow, 5).Value = "Memory Used (kb)"
    .Cells(CountRow, 6).Value = "Missing Items Limit"
    .Cells(CountRow, 7).Value = "Record Count"
    .Cells(CountRow, 8).Value = "Refresh Date"
```

```
      .Cells(CountRow, 9).Value = "Refresh Period"
      .Cells(CountRow, 10).Value = "Source Data File"
      .Cells(CountRow, 11).Value = "Source Type"
      .Rows(1).EntireRow.Font.Bold = True
   End With

   CountRow = CountRow + 1

      For Each pc In wb.PivotCaches
        With ws
          On Error Resume Next
          .Cells(CountRow, 1).Value = pc.Index
          .Cells(CountRow, 2).Value = pc.CommandText
          .Cells(CountRow, 3).Value = pc.CommandType
          .Cells(CountRow, 4).Value = pc.Connection
          .Cells(CountRow, 5).Value = pc.MemoryUsed / 1000
          .Cells(CountRow, 6).Value = pc.MissingItemsLimit
          .Cells(CountRow, 7).Value = pc.RecordCount
          .Cells(CountRow, 8).Value = pc.RefreshDate
          .Cells(CountRow, 9).Value = pc.RefreshPeriod
          .Cells(CountRow, 10).Value = pc.SourceDataFile
          .Cells(CountRow, 11).Value = pc.SourceType
        End With
        CountRow = CountRow + 1
      Next pc

End Sub
```

To run the code, use a method described in Section 13.1. The code refers to ActiveWorkbook, so you can run the code on any workbook that contains a pivot table.

How It Works

The ListPivotCacheInfo macro deletes the Cache_Info sheet, if one exists. Then, it adds a new sheet, and names it Cache_Info. Headings are entered in the first row of the new sheet, and details on the workbook caches are listed in the following rows.

13.24. Resetting the Print Area to Include the Entire Pivot Table

Problem

Your pivot table is on a worksheet that contains other data. The pivot table frequently changes size, and you have to reset the print area every time you want to print it.

Solution

Use programming to reset the print area automatically before printing. Add the following code to a regular code module:

```
Sub SetPivotPrintArea()
Dim ws As Worksheet
Dim pt As PivotTable

  Set ws = ActiveSheet
  Set pt = ws.PivotTables(1)

  With ws.PageSetup
    .PrintTitleRows = ""
    .PrintTitleColumns = ""
    .PrintArea = pt.TableRange2.Address
  End With

  pt.PrintTitles = True
  ws.PrintOut Preview:=True

End Sub
```

To run the code, use a method described in Section 13.1. The code refers to ActiveSheet, so you can run the code on any sheet that contains a pivot table.

How It Works

The SetPivotPrintArea macro clears the print titles for the active sheet, sets the print area based on the current layout of the pivot table, turns on the pivot table's print titles options, and prints the worksheet. In this example, the ws.PrintOut line has Preview set to True, so the worksheet will preview instead of printing. When you've finished testing the code, you can change the setting to False, and the sheet will print when the code runs.

13.25. Printing the Pivot Table for Each Page Field

Problem

You want to print a copy of the pivot table for each page in your Pivot table.

Solution

The following code will print the pivot table once for each item in the first page field. Store the code in a regular code module.

```
Sub PrintPivotPages()
    Dim pt As PivotTable
    Dim pf As PivotField
    Dim pi As PivotItem
    Dim ws As Worksheet
    On Error Resume Next

    Set ws = ActiveSheet
    Set pt = ws.PivotTables(1)
    Set pf = pt.PageFields(1)

    For Each pi In pf.PivotItems
      pt.PivotFields(pf.Name).CurrentPage = pi.Name
      ws.PrintOut Preview:=True
    Next pi
End Sub
```

To run the code, use a method described in Section 13.1. The code refers to ActiveSheet, so you can run the code on any sheet that contains a pivot table.

How It Works

The PrintPivotPages macro selects each item in the pivot table's first page field, then prints the worksheet. In this example, the ws.PrintOut line has Preview set to True, so the worksheet will preview instead of printing. When you've finished testing the code, you can change the setting to False, and the sheet will print when the code runs.

Notes

The procedure can be modified slightly to print a copy of a pivot chart on a chart sheet for each item in the first page field. Store the code on a regular code module.

```
Sub PrintPivotChartPages()
  Dim pt As PivotTable
  Dim pf As PivotField
  Dim pi As PivotItem
  Dim ch As Chart
  On Error Resume Next

  Set ch = ActiveChart
  Set pt = ch.PivotLayout.PivotTable
  Set pf = pt.PageFields(1)

  For Each pi In pf.PivotItems
    pt.PivotFields(pf.Name).CurrentPage = pi.Name
    ch.PrintOut Preview:=True
  Next pi
End Sub
```

13.26. Reformatting Pivot Charts After Changing the Pivot Table

Problem

When you refresh the pivot table on which the pivot chart is based, the series formatting in the chart is lost.

Solution

You can record a macro as you format the pivot chart series. Then, run the macro after changing the pivot table.

To run the macro automatically, you can use the PivotTableUpdate event to trigger it. For example, to run a recorded procedure named ReformatChart when the pivot table is changed, store the following code on the pivot table's worksheet module:

```
Private Sub Worksheet_PivotTableUpdate(ByVal Target As PivotTable)
  ReformatChart
End Sub
```

To run the code, refresh or change the pivot table.

How It Works

The PivotTableUpdate event procedure runs the ReformatChart macro that contains your recorded code to reformat the pivot chart.

13.27. Scrolling Through Page Field Items on a Pivot Chart

Problem

You have a long list of customers in the Pivot Chart page field. Instead of selecting the next customer from the dropdown list to view its chart, you'd like scrolling buttons on the chart so you can quickly view each customer's data.

Solution

You can add buttons from the Forms toolbar, and assign a macro to each button, then click the buttons to select the next or previous page field item.

1. Add the following two procedures to a regular code module:

```
Sub PivotPageNext()
  Dim CountPI As Long
  Dim i As Long
  Dim pt As PivotTable
  Dim pf As PivotField
  Dim pi As PivotItem

  Set pt = ActiveChart.PivotLayout.PivotTable
  Set pf = pt.PageFields(1)
  CountPI = 1
  i = 1

  For Each pi In pf.PivotItems
    If pf.CurrentPage.Name = "(All)" Then
      CountPI = 0
      Exit For
    End If
    If pi.Name = pf.CurrentPage.Name Then
        Exit For
    End If
    CountPI = CountPI + 1
  Next pi

  For i = CountPI + 1 To pf.PivotItems.Count + 1
    On Error Resume Next
```

```
      If i = pf.PivotItems.Count + 1 Then
        pf.CurrentPage = "(All)"
        Exit For
      End If
      pf.CurrentPage = pf.PivotItems(i).Name
        If Err.Number = 0 Then
          Exit For
        End If
    Next i
End Sub

Sub PivotPagePrev()
  Dim CountPI As Long
  Dim i As Long
  Dim pt As PivotTable
  Dim pf As PivotField
  Dim pi As PivotItem

  Set pt = ActiveChart.PivotLayout.PivotTable
  Set pf = pt.PageFields(1)
  CountPI = 1

  For Each pi In pf.PivotItems
    If pf.CurrentPage.Name = "(All)" Then
      CountPI = pf.PivotItems.Count + 1
      Exit For
    End If
    If pi.Name = pf.CurrentPage.Name Then Exit For
    CountPI = CountPI + 1
  Next pi

  For i = CountPI - 1 To 0 Step -1
    On Error Resume Next
    pf.CurrentPage = pf.PivotItems(i).Name
      If Err.Number = 0 Then Exit For
    If i = 0 Then
      pf.CurrentPage = "(All)"
      Exit For
    End If
  Next i
End Sub
```

2. On the Excel worksheet menu, choose View ➤ Toolbars ➤ Forms.

3. On the Forms toolbar, use the Button tool to add two buttons at the top of the pivot chart sheet. For the first button, when the Assign Macro dialog box appears, select PivotPagePrev. For the second button, select PivotPageNext.

4. Right-click each button, and select Edit Text. On the first button, type **<Prev** and on the second button type **Next>** (see Figure 13-7).

5. To scroll through the page field items, click the <Prev or Next> button.

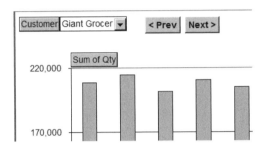

Figure 13-7. *Scrolling buttons at the top of a pivot chart*

How It Works

The two macros check the current page field item and calculate its position in the list of items. If the <Prev button is clicked, the PivotPagePrev macro runs, and the visible item with the next lower number is shown. If the Next> button is clicked, the PivotPageNext macro runs, and the visible item with the next higher number is shown.

Index

Find it faster at http://superindex.apress.com/

You Need the Companion eBook

Your purchase of this book entitles you to its companion eBook for only $10.

We believe this Apress title will prove so indispensable that you'll want to carry it with you everywhere, which is why we are offering the companion eBook for $10 to customers who purchase this book now. Convenient and fully searchable, the eBook version of any content-rich, page-heavy Apress book makes a valuable addition to your programming library. You can easily find, copy, and apply code—and then perform examples by quickly toggling between instructions and the application. Even simultaneously tackling a donut, diet soda, and complex code becomes simplified with hands-free eBooks!

Once you purchase this book, getting the $10 companion eBook is simple:

❶ Visit **www.apress.com/promo/tendollars/**.

❷ Complete a basic registration form to receive a randomly generated question about this title.

❸ Answer the question correctly in 60 seconds and you will receive a promotional code to redeem for the $10 eBook.

2560 Ninth Street • Suite 219 • Berkeley, CA 94710

Offer valid through 9/6/06.